LINE

OF

WEALTH

LINE OF WEALTH

A justice based economy on based on the new approach for Line of Wealth

Roshan Lal Agarwal

White Falcon Publishing

www.whitefalconpublishing.com

Line of Wealth
Roshan Lal Agarwal
Edited by Zulfiqar Shah

www.whitefalconpublishing.com

ISBN - 978-93-89085-56-3

CONTENTS

CHAPTER 1

DESIRE FOR PEACE

No one wants to remain in trouble or peril. Everyone desires peace and comfort; however this basic dream of people still remains unfulfilled. Whether physics, spirituality or any other fields of knowledge, all have shown unimaginable advancement, yet the vast expansion of knowledge and research have made people more restless and miserable.

Physics. It has caused unimaginable comforts to humans. Because of technological invention many impossible or hard works have become easy. This branch of science has unveiled the secret of skies and oceans. Today, we have knowledge of many aspects of space as well as ocean. Despite all these developments, human beings are still yearning for peace and prosperity. Scientific advancement has made no contribution in this regards.

Meanwhile, the developments in science have upside downed the social, economical and political system and human life. Nothing has escaped the change. The conventional communication -- land, air and sea transportation -- has drastically changed. We can travel easily today, one destination to another, in airplane, train and cars.

With the help of different means and modes of transportation, heavy goods can be delivered from one end of earth to the other. Similarly the discoveries of radio, television and internet have changed everything in the field of information and communication. Besides, production boosting tools and equipments have become norm in the industry as well as agriculture. Hard laboured work has become simplified with latest technologies. A work which needed hundreds of people previously is replaced by the labour of a few today. This has enhanced production tremendously though rarely the production has surpassed the demand.

Traffic and transportation has increased along with the trade, and has become global. Products from across the world are being sold everywhere. This, no doubt, was unimaginable previously. For their business and work some industrialists, traders and politicians travel thousands of kilometres in one day, complete their work in different countries and return home by the evening. They have breakfast in one country, lunch in other, dinner in third and take rest in the fourth country.

Advancement in telecommunications has greatly influenced the way people interact with each other globally. Today, individuals and businessmen can interact easily through audio-visual call and data sharing applications. The physical distance is evaded by the virtual connectivity. Traditional telephony and transistor have become obsolete, cellular and television communication has replaced them. They help access us to the information and happenings around the world.

Internet has made our life easier and more convenient. We can use internet to communicate with the people around the world; do business, make new friend and know different cultures; find information and analysis; and study also. The internet does not only enable us communication through email but also ensures easy availability of information, images, and products amongst other things. The internet can let a person communicate with people virtually in any part of the world without having to leave his room. Email allows people to communicate in fraction of time. It is now possible to send a message to any parts of the world through an e-mail and the message is delivered within seconds. Every company use email for business communications. The convenience of email has allowed businesses to expand, and to communicate with their supplier, vendors as well as customers located all over the world. Personal communication has also become easier, thanks to email! Chat rooms and video conferencing are some of the latest additions in this technology and these have allowed peoples to chat in real time. The internet also allows people within an organization to easily communicate and share information.

Information through websites is the biggest advantage that internet offers. Internet is a virtual treasures trove of information. There is a huge amount of information available on the internet which so many is not even available in the biggest libraries.

LINE OF WEALTH

The crux of the matter is that inventions in physics have completely changed all aspects of human life. It has completely changed human lifestyle, and thinking. The things that were previously impossible have become possible and easy today. Science has provided vast facilities for comfort and peace, yet peace and comfort is distancing from human life. A person is usual victim of everyday uproars and confrontations, and has become restless, confused, depressed as well as insecure.

Scientific inventions have not only increased confrontation but also polluted environment. Soil, water and air have become badly affected and have become serious danger for human life. The ozone layer which is considered as protective layer of earth has been disastrously damaged. The disease that earlier was limited to certain areas can now spread across the world. Manufacturing various kinds of lethal weapons and tendency to hoard them, as well as their use in a commoner's life is increasing. The invention of latest equipments for spying and way to use them has badly infringed the personal life. The dark shadow of fear and anger is making everyone fearful. Cooperation, amity and trust are vanishing fast. The incidents of murder, suicide, crime, conspiracy and terrorism are rising. Nobody knows when the confrontations will turn into wars.

Increase in material facilities has turned people their slaves. This has enhanced accumulation of wealth. The growing greed in people has reduced the space for non-narrow and liberal thinking in the society. People are getting more and more selfish and narrow minded. Human generosity and broader morality is becoming extinct. The desire for more wealth coupled with modern developments has turned persons blind to cognize suffering and injustice done with others. The trade of human organs, fatal drugs, narcotics and illegal weapons has become means to acquire huge wealth in short span of time.

Despite huge production and supply of goods, people across the world are continued to suffer due to hunger, scarcity of resources, misery and exploitation. Poverty has forced a large section of world population to spend life of an animal. They are simply deprived of the basic needs. Even thoughtful people are compelled to criminal activities due to hunger and poverty. It is marathon to amass money. The excessive production is being destroyed instead of being given to the needful. Some burn food items, while others throw out milk and other dairy products into rivers and seas. They do this to ensure that prices of these goods do not decline in the markets. It is to continue earning profit.

Instead of noticing these harmful developments and tendencies, nations neglect or promote various practices in their interest. The obsession to collect and amass wealth has become so dominant that the peoples' needs and necessities forgotten. They have forgotten the universality of death. Such persons desire to enhance their power to the extent where people are compelled to follow them. The rush to accumulate wealth and power is destroying humanity. A group of riches and powerful want to hostage and enslave people of the world.

The gist is the luxuries and wealth have created hardships for the people. They are paying heavy price for the facilities they are getting. They are instructed by the competitors and enemies. Uncertainty, doubt and mistrust have surrounded them. They are like a fearful person crossing the thick jungle amid the dangerous animals where he or she can prey victim of the beasts – the traveller may be composed apparently but in fact would be fearful and restless. The dream for real comfort and peace is yet unfulfilled.

CHAPTER 2
SURVIVAL

Everyone wishes to spend a happy and peaceful life and wants to remain happy forever. Nobody requires interference in his pleasures and does not anticipate any suffering. He or she wants to spend a free and fearless life regarding life and property. One wishes individually that every object of need as well as niche stand fulfilled utmost with little effort.

Constant consumption is needed for survival. No one can survive without bread, cloth and house (*Hindi/Urdu: Roti, Kapda, Makan*). Human beings get all these from the natural resources. To have substances for human consumption – the consumables -- a person does not only work hard but work more to make it worth utilized. Hard work accompanies pain and consumes energy. Without hard work, one has to face shortage of consumable. The precious resources meant for consumption are produced by nature. They also decay, however. Consumables often scarce. They availability reduce after utilization. In order to avoid scarcity troubles, every person intend to stockpile additional quantity of consumables. This is a common practice in today's market driven economy to meet current as well future consumptions and avoid adversaries caused by the scarcity or extinction of consumables.

Uncertainty is root cause behind hoarding o large sale purchase of consumables. Besides, a person has also learnt to produce various consumables through entirely new and different means a few human resources if compared with natural or traditional technique of production. This fundamentally requires land. Therefore, everyone wants to establish a monopoly on the land to produce consumables. Everyone desires stockpile consumables to whatsoever extent possible ensuring maximum happiness.

Simultaneously, the stockpile of one causes or can cause misery to other(s), because almost all consumables can be consumed in limited duration of time. Therefore, a manmade scarcity is created for many. Therefore, two options – to work hard or to face the scarcity exist eventually. This gives birth to agony and conflict of interest that leads to war. The victors become owners of means of productions and losers become dependent. They are also evicted and sometimes are turned into real or virtual slaves. An unending struggle for owning land and other means of production begins. The losers resurge to revenge and battle to win this war of interest again. War claims lives and assets, hence it always cause miseries.

Finally the biggest obstacle in the human path to live happy and in peace is the clash of interest between two or more. This conflict cannot be avoided without war or struggle around the interest. The main reason in almost every conflict is economic disparity. A peaceful solution of this lies only in a justice that is for all.

CHAPTER 3

ECONOMIC JUSTICE

Economic Justice has derived from two terms – economy and justice. Economy, the first part of the term is related to wealth. Consumables and consumption is a process in an economy, and saved consumables or their value results in accumulation of wealth. The second part of the term is Justice, which is niche in a conflict whether between individuals or among group(s). The virtue of a consensus in the conflicts is justice. The usual point of agreement in the process of conflict resolution use to be justice. On the basis of mutual agreement, any conflict or differences can be resolved peacefully. Such agreement, however, should be reached upon without any fear, greed, pressure or ignorance. Only the agreement based on truth can sustain.

The very idea of justice is social, which is a result of social experience and thought of human. The law of jungle is the determining factor for the ownership of the natural resources around a fight between two animals, for instance, the powerful either kills the weaker one or defeat him. Hence, this is called law of jungle or injustice. Therefore, power should not interfere in the process of justice in a bid to let truth and justice prevail. The foundation of justice is equality. In the human justice, the meaning of Economic Justice is a situation where every human being has equal share on the natural resources. It is not based on the talent, aptitude or effort. It is just beyond that. Economic justice is a fundamental human right, and cannot be violated. On the foothold of this rights regime, a person's right on the wealth can tangibly be measured in a ceiling on the wealth that fall in the fundamental right sphere. The possession of wealth more than the ceiling should be considered outside the fundamental right. This ceiling on the wealth is the average Line of Wealth, and simply can be called average right on the wealth. Any other unequal rights, possession or ownership on the natural resource is injustice.

One can retain more than average line of wealth. On the basis of justice, average line of wealth can be calculated when somebody has more than line of wealth while others have lesser.

The assets above an average line of wealth are excessive wealth that can be attained by the humans without doing significant labour or efforts. On the basis of justice that wealth should also be distributed among those who are unemployed, illiterate, and incompetent or simply does to those play a productive role in the society.

Hence, on the basis of justice everyone should have freedom to earn wealth on the basis of competence and efforts and should have all rights to use that wealth. While counting the average line of wealth, it must be kept in mind that only surplus wealth more than consumption of an individual should be included. Everyone, indeed, should have freedom to use wealth of natural resources according to the need. The problem arises when someone due to his competence and efforts earn more wealth than that of his need thereby accumulates the wealth. Since the natural resources used to consume at a time remain in limited quantity, therefore the less competent persons are unable to have their part of wealth. If the people with more competence get the resources for their consumption according to their need only, then the weak people will have recourses according to their need as well.

Therefore, the question arises whether a person should be deprived of the wealth to establish the economic justice? This is neither appropriate nor beneficial and practical. It is also opposite to the common human psych. A just and best path is required in this direction. Social wellbeing cannot be realized by rejecting the truth.

While considering all the prior questions, first of all we should also consider the role or utility of wealth. People use natural resources in two ways: one, using the necessary ingredients for consumption to maintain life; two, creating ancillary resources for reducing the labour needed to acquire production out of natural resources.

Availability of various types of consumables that are directly consumed is also an issue. Many consumables use to be available and can be produced within a short span of time in days or months. Gradually their availability decreases. Therefore, when they are available abundantly, they can easily be obtained. If they are not stored, they become inconsumable and thereby discarded or they are consumed by other creatures. These are utilized in certain cases for by-production out of these inconsumable produces. Thus, human requires storing them for present and the future. Meanwhile, the accumulation of wealth in its origin has embryos in storing resources due to future uncertainty. Man can only accumulate more money than that of his requirement for consumption in better times. In adversaries, he or she becomes unable earning enough money to meet the basic needs. Thus, one accumulates wealth to avoid probable future impoverishment.

Another important reason for accumulation of wealth is the means of production that are used basically for produce out of natural resources. The phenomenon reduces the human labor and increase quantity of produce, which has become today's goal. This is based on scientific and technological advancements. The technologies are used for long period and thereafter are recycled. Such equipments have boosted the human capacity as well capability. They perform hard and impossible tasks. In terms of human, social and structural performance, almost all social, economic and political systems are operating through the technologies. Their increase, reduce the human role and strength. In final result, accumulation of wealth is directly proportionate to the scale and quantum of the technology use. If one does not accumulate wealth, one is deprived of benefits through modern technologies.

The justification for accumulation of wealth is always expressed in eligibility and capacity versus incompetence. In general, the capacity of labour in human is great enough to earn more money than their requirement if they are given freedoms and rights. To the limited scale, some cannot earn their consumables despites freedoms and rights as well abundance of natural resources. In economic justice, a balance can be created by removing the imbalances caused by the excuse of competence versus incompetence; however this requires a ceiling on the savings -- a common word for accumulation of wealth.

Having no right to accumulate wealth beyond the average ceiling, the line of wealth, would be an injustice to the competent persons that would no doubt lead to a huge loss to the society. If we think of prosperity in the society, the competent persons can rightly use the means of production and thus get more produce. Therefore, the nature of the arrangements should be the competent rightfully use the means of production in a bid to get maximum output. They should be given exclusive rewards for their output since there competence also contributes in the society. This will also enrich the entire society and everyone will be satisfied.

Possessing more than line of wealth violates the fundamental wealth rights of weaker or less competent persons, therefore, one part of such wealth should be redistributed among them as social compensation; however rest of the wealth may remain to the accumulator. Besides, accumulation of wealth beyond the average line or ceiling should not violate the fundamental right to the wealth.

Essentially, justice has two foundations -- equality and freedom. Neither equality, nor freedom alone can be justice. Both are pillars of justice. Equality without freedom causes selfishness and pseudo egoism. Freedom without equality results slavery. Harmony between freedom and equality is the condition. If we want to understand justice in depth, we must understand interrelation between equality and freedom. They are in harmony as well as opposite to each other simultaneously. Without economic justice, where there is freedom, there cannot be equality and vice versa. In the line of establishing economic justice, we need to accept both along with their realities and importance. Coupled with human will, freedom and equality can build a meaningful economy and prosperous as well as peaceful society. This is the sole path to the salvation from poverty, scarcity, exploitation, slavery, injustice, crime, unemployment, corruption, Naxalism[1] and terrorism and much more.

---

1 A decades long armed conflict between government forces and Naxalism activists in India claiming Marxist ideology; however have failed to bring socialist revolution even in one district

CHAPTER 4
LINE OF WEALTH

In India, the nation today undergoes vast economic disparity. Mostly, the largest volume of the assets in the country is usurped by a few affluent persons, meanwhile the rest; majority population is compelled to live in extreme poverty and *wealthless*. The rich has legal possession and dominancy on all means of production like in trade, industry and agriculture. Most of the benefits of the economy go to the multi-millionaires. They live luxurious and their wealth increase continuously. Hence, vast majority is devoid of wealth due to their limited earnings. There exists income difference and gap between two groups – haves and have-nots. This difference and gap have further widened to the extent that rich becomes richer and poor becomes poorer.

This injustice is destroying entire system of society. As the unjust economic inequality is increasing, the problem of distrust, dissatisfaction, confrontation and rebellion against the system also getting increasingly complex and even taking destructive turn. Naxalism, terrorism, separatism, as well as heinous and organized crimes are just a reflection of anger against such unjust system.

Those who consider them as law and order problem are either stupid or cunning. Employment opportunities are continuously decreasing and the crowd of unemployed is constantly increasing. As the unemployment is increases, also increase the rage. All forms of wealth and all high positions of power that are constitutional office holding of the country have been usurped by the most selfish, cunning, hypocrites, criminal or dishonest people. They are plundering together the entire society, and also misguiding it.

A question rise again and again that what exactly are the basic causes of these problems, and can there be any solution? A social order is basically a comprehensive agreement as well as arrangement that aim to complement each other by establishing a fair consensus in the interest of all people. Most of the conflicts in the society are economy related because the basic need of a person is diet, cloths and housing. In a just economy, all the needs of people can be fulfilled smoothly. Meanwhile, if a system is not based on justice, it will certainly lead the society towards chaos, conflict and violence. An uneven economic system is the sole cause of these and many other problems. Therefore, to achieve the goal of happiness, prosperity and beauty, primarily economic construct of the society should be formed on just and fair foundations. People accept a system only when it benefits them. In a just society mutual cooperation exists, while in an unjust society chaos takes place in the name of competition. Today, everyone is employed according to the ability as well as interest therefore performance and production is upscale and hard labour becomes a passion. However, the sustainable achievements and successes of the system can only contain when surplus benefits are redistributed on the basis of economic justice. It just not mere sharing benefits among all. Hence, resentment, mistrust, unemployment, poverty, exploitation, violence, crime and conspiracy thrive. Eventually, the non-existence of distribution of surplus profit among all; and unfair economic system are the basis of the economic disparity.

In order to establish justice, all aspects of socio-political economy need to be rethought. Justice is all citizens have equal rights on natural resources of a country. Human persons have this right since the birth.

Wealth rights should have ceiling up to an average extent of property holding. It is unjust to allow ceiling free ownership of wealth without being especially taxed on the basis of on the line of wealth concept. Secondly, in terms of social and governance practices, tailoring one's fundamental rights on the basis of competence or any other specialty is a jungle rule. In terms of justice, no matter how much a person is qualified or talented, maximum extent of his authority must be determined. The system does not recognize a ceiling regarding one's wealth rights. This kicks off accumulation of wealth associated with concentration of power, making the poor and weaker a powerless without wealth. It is necessary to determine the ceiling for the property ownership rights of a person because after inclusion of technology in the process of production and services, which will also play a very important role in market process. Production today does not largely depend only on human labour. Modern technology makes production easily and swift and voluminous in comparison with the pure human labor based production generation. In fact, due to scientific and technological advancements, the entire social system has become dependent of technology.

The inventions in science and technology have changed the means of production and ways to exchange produce and commodities. Today the role of technology has become more important turning human labor almost worthless. Decline in the role of labor has led to poverty, unemployment and exploitation of the people dependent of wages from physical labour. It is clearly demonstrated that the wealth of the people is now increasing not because of their competence, strength or labor, but because of the technology use.

Continuous accumulation of wealth is on the toe by the some. This, a very alarming and dangerous situation, can devastate social fabric. Making a just and happy society, the momentous is to adopt Line of Wealth instead of a much touted Line of Poverty indicator for economic development. On the basis of justice, the maximum rights of the competent persons and minimum rights of incompetent or incapable persons should be defined. Without this, the basic rights of the poor and weak persons cannot be protected. In fact, the system always faces threat by the competent and powerful. Therefore measuring economy and development on the indicator of line of poverty line is ignorance or deception with the society.

It has become necessary to draw a 'line of wealth' because advancement of science and new innovations, inventions and powerful technologies are replacing human labour in almost all kinds of production. Hence employment based on human labour is steadily decreasing. The final outcome will be an end of the employment based on human labour. Because of modern technology there will be enough production to meet human needs across the globe. What, then, will become of those who become jobless due to this phenomenon? They will not be earning their daily life. A horrific situation indeed! It is social and humanitarian responsibility of people of the world to address this situation.

What is the percentile of such people whose livelihood is based on human labour? A single person is able today to manage huge production using modern technology. In yesteryears, this required a large number of workers; however mere 10 to 12 percent of those are employed for that today. In a more advanced technologies tomorrow, fewer human laborers will be employed for production. Roughly mere 5 to 10 percent laborers can produce what in past has been produced by the 100. In that scenario, ninety percent of people will have no source of income and they will ineligible to work. A frightening human tragedy we are about to undergo. This also will also impact rich, because when the mostly jobless world population will cause reduction in purchasing power everywhere hence consumption will decline. It is speculated that ninety percent of the world population will face hunger, and markets will be deserted. An economic and social anarchy will rule everywhere.

The best and equitable remedy to avoid all these horrible situations is to adopt Line of Wealth Line approach. As mentioned earlier, on the basis of justice, a man should have the right to freedom of property only to an extent of a median ceiling of wealth, which is considered to be the fundamental right on property. Possessing more wealth than that of line of wealth, an owner should be considered a manager of wealth, who is indebted to the society for having more than legal ceiling for the wealth. All natural resources and property are owned by society, indeed! In case a competent person earns and thereby accumulates more wealth due to his competence, such accumulation in fact reduces consumables as well as property for the rest if seen in totality. It is a violation of fundamental rights of the people.

A competent person should have freedom to earn whatsoever extent one can; however he should not be the sole owner of every asset he accumulates or buy through it without paying a significant amount on it to the society – a collective. Since natural resources can be transformed but created, therefore one cannot have sole ownership and authorization on everything one accumulates. Hence, a quantum of labor utilized for earning should considered a ceiling and whatsoever form of possession may only be allowed. The remaining possessed property should be forwarded to the real owner which is the commoner. Understanding this, the *Bataidari System* (sharecropping) in India can be the best example. It is an agricultural practice where a landowner lends his land to another mostly peasant who spends money and labour on it and the produce is shared by the owner and the tenant equally. This sharing of produce also include the accounting the expenditure on the cultivation. An owner is not laborer always. He gets his share from the production due to ownership or possession. Therefore, both should also be regarded as the shareholders of that wealth.

A citizen should be entitled the property up to a ceiling, and a tax should be levied at the fixed rate of interest if someone holding more assets then that of average ceiling. The levied taxes can also be called rent or royalty of holding extra wealth. Taxation at fixed rate of interest is justified because a person will get benefits from the natural resources, not of the human labor. All other types of taxes should be abolished and a one-tax system should be introduced. Revenues through one-tax system on wealth above the ceiling should be utilized for government expenditure as well as distributed equally among all citizens of country.

By this, the economy will not only get rid of different types of anomalies, distortions, difficulties, obstacles, ambiguities, contradictions and dishonesty, but also the people will get their fair share from the benefits of taxation on excessive wealth too. With this, every person will get a source of income to spend a life with dignity. It will also be the simplest solution to the complex human and social problems arising due to the unemployment and other similar situations. It will further empower the commoner. It will also create a very high demand for the commodities and produces in the market. Resultantly, there will be a huge demand for workforce in agriculture, dairy, industry and business of all kinds and services. They will be able to sell their production at their own price making huge economic benefit. With the elimination of different types of taxes, increase will be observed in production, demand and consumption due to decrease in prices therefore it will not cause any damage, upside-down or recession in the economy. Instead due to increased demand and cheaper production, the economic volume will enhance. The governments and managements will also get rid of plenty of account books, bills and vouchers. It will also end the discrimination, humiliation and extortions done by rulers and administrators with the others. People will involve their inputs and efforts in the work with more commitment and honesty.

A suitable ecology to utilize competence freely will help support people to work towards a better society. Everyone will be self-sufficient, and will be able to choose his or her role according to the ability, qualification and interests. Caste, sect, gender, language and professional discrimination will end. Everyone will be sustainably secure. None will have to do any unwanted or unreasonable work to earn livelihood. The trend of exploitation will get curbed. No person in a country will be victim of helplessness, poverty or injustice. Nobody will be compelled for begging, theft, narcotics addiction due to frustration, and prostitution. A reduction in the liquor consumption will reduces the quantity of sell and numbers of liquor vendors. Prosperity will be across the board. New economic heights will be the destination. There will be an atmosphere of mutual goodwill, cooperation, faith and satisfaction. It will also reduce the greed for accumulation of wealth and consumables. Citizens support the system and governments will be backed due to such a best practices. The tendencies of Naxalism terrorism, crime and other violations will reduce. Unity and love will be the stronger social bonds. Destruction of nature will stop. Earth will be free from environmental crises. The population in the cities will reduce, and the deserted villages will not only get developed but appropriately settled also.

CHAPTER 5

AN IDEAL ECONOMY

An ideal economy is when all means of production together meet the needs of people. However there requires an ultimate balance between production and use/consumption. In short, production should be directly proportionate with the total need. Surplus production is unsustainable as well as unsuitable for environment and ecology because it leads to the overuse and misuse of natural resources and cause social and environmental hazards. A human person should have freedom to decide his or her scope of abilities and interests. Everyone should have the unalienable opportunity to develop his or her capability. Economic inequality of any sort should not violate the iternal principle of justice. Countries should not allow the accumulation of wealth based on disproportionate means of production. An economy must be transparent, plural and balanced. No motivation should be allowed leading persons towards unfair mean of earning.

In order to establish an ideal economy, we must understand the principle of economic mobility. The smooth monetary circulation in all forms and aspects will help support healthy and prosperous society. The monitory mobility/circulation or simply mobility of money can be resembled with the cycle of water in the fresh water bodies. Oceans are the largest water bodies, many fresh water rivers and tributaries submerge with it, and keep on its filling, but there is no significance increase in the oceanic water level. Although due to climate change, particularly rise in temperature, glacial melt has increased the level of the seas, which is because human has went against nature and thus changed the cycle of water on the earth. In the natural cycle, temperature use to evaporate the seawater which in turns creates clouds and finally water through clouds returns back to the plains, mountains and deserts. This can be called cycle to green earth and support life on it. In the conclusive end, the very same waters fill sea through rivers, basins and deltas, and on-ground water resources. Meanwhile, the portion of that rain creates sub-soil water reservoirs on one hand culminates in the sea or works as natural balance for the life. Oceans and clouds have no scarcity of water. The circulation of money also has similar cycle. It constantly changes its form.

Extraction from the natural resources ideally should be done according to the human need. Such extraction is transformed and presented into various forms to meet the human needs. Economic actions of all sorts whether agricultural or industrial are similar to water cycle. The economic activities profit mere rich, unlike the natural cycle of the water, and does not trickle down to the poor and weaker sections of the society. Therefore, wealth is accumulated in monetary terms by the rich, while rest are devoid of it. Although money while accumulated becomes a commodity but it is not available to the majority according to their consumption need. A left out of this cycle has no choice to earn suitable income. This has resulted into drastic reduction in purchasing power and market demand badly affecting industrial, trade, agriculture, and livestock economy. Recessions are born out of it. On one hand overproduction and hoarding is a challenge a large number of people is facing hunger in the world. The phenomenon is disastrous for both the economy and the society.

It is a flaw-full economy today. It has imbalance in structural organism. An economy usually has four aspects --production, exchange, distribution, and consumption. It aims to produce the maximum with minimum labour so that the product should reach maximum people for consumption. Production and consumption together is orbit of economy, while exchange and distribution are supplementary. Essentially the production and consumption have to be directly proportionate; however consumption is based on need. Therefore, it should be according to the need. The misbalance in production for human needs is due to uncontrolled producers as well as production trends, which ultimately leave negative impacts on society. Quantity of production does matter, higher or lesser it has to effect population. .

Therefore, following an 'economic cycle' similar to the prior expressed natural cycle of water, is the sustainable solution to many problems. In this regards line of wealth should be adopted as key parameter for economic development like hitherto the prosperity of a nations is measured through the line of poverty. Justice is only when there is ceiling on possession of wealth based on a midline drawn from a nation's economy. On the very same line, there should be a ceiling of 'average wealth'. There needs to be ceiling on wealth possession. A new tax regime of one-tax system should be introduced by taxing the wealth that one possesses beyond the ceiling – a line of wealth. Such taxation should encompass the possession of all forms of wealth in accordance with their market value. The revenues generated from one-tax system should be a kind of royalty for the citizens on the excessive wealth that surpass the ceiling. This royalty has to be charged in larger amount to trickle into down to the people. The hitherto unrealized development has to take place through this alone.

Such an economy will have profound and greater impact on the entire society. Disparity in the form of rich-poor gap will continuously reduce; and both will mutually engage with respecting each other, thus a new society will emerge. The society will consider rich the one who pays royalty to them on their excessive property and wealth. Poor will have financial security. They will finally have the freedom. They will contribute more to the society, which will be the reason of their bliss. Even a smaller number among the poor involved in crime and gimmicks will also engage in the process of production and services. Trust will prevail in every corporate or business entity beyond the class background of employees', which will evade concerns of the employer. A healthy soul, mind and body will prevail everywhere. Poor will not face dearth of consumables. They will not also be ill-treated. A happy and pleasant society will exist. Significant reduction in crime rate as well as conflicts will be ensured. Equitable economic cohesion can be a basis for sustainable unity, peace, harmony, cooperation, trust, prosperity and security in the society.

The rich and competent persons must understand that they will receive collective respect only when they benefit the entire society. A society should be compared with the human organism. Like a health body is essential, a healthy society requires healthy social being.

Issues make one selfish and greedy. In bid to keep a people happy, such human tilts need to be discouraged and curbed. The Line of Wealth approach in practice is also necessary check to the greed -- the accumulation of wealth. This also will set a climax for economic cycle, and ultimately will lead to a prosperous society. This will create a new bond of trust among the people/persons. In fact, a balanced production and consumption equation will work that will create a sustainable economy, human development and ecology. World finally will get rid of the unpredicted recessions in every country. A full stop to unemployment and poverty will be greatest human achievement due to this. Self-reliant and independent human persons finally will become reality of our human history. Ability and competence will further groom. In a society where all will be wise, equipped with the knowledge and health, will finally defeat the illiteracy and superstations.

CHAPTER 6

EMANCIPATION FROM SCARCITY

One of the fundamental purposes of the economic management is to free the society from scarcity that ultimately means everyone in a society should be prosperous and free form any shortage of consumables, production and services.

The competent in a society should get profit and benefit no doubt; however the lagged-behind-ones, disadvantaged and disables should also get benefit out of competents' efforts. All these objectives can be easily attained by adopting Line of Wealth approach. Because of such taxation, only 1 to1.2 million most prosperous citizens in India will have to pay tax, and rest shall become un-taxed.

Based on Line of Wealth which is a ceiling on the wealth possession, a one-tax system should be adopted consisting abolition of all other taxes and introducing one-tax on the wealth above the ceiling decided for everyone. The revenues of one-tax system will be ten times more than what are current tax receipts per annum; meanwhile payees will be handfuls of rich.

In fact, 70-75 percent of total private property in India is owned by 1 - 1.2 million rich through property rights laws. They are 0.1 percent of India's 1.25 billion population; while 99.9 percent population possesses 25- 30 percent private property. By taxing 1 to 1.2 million wealthy through one-tax system around 2 trillion Indian Rupees (INR) per annum revenues will generate. Central and State governments in India today have annual revenue from citizens of INR 250 to 300 million. Deficit budgets are common phenomena due to which Indian economy suffers.

Let's summarize the economic, social, political, cultural, moral and human connotations of social issues and their solutions in India.

- Liberation from taxes on citizens: Everyone is taxed on consumptions, services and fundamental human needs like bread, cloths, houses, education, health and justice. If current taxation is replaced with one-tax system, everyone would be well off and realize real human liberty.
- Inflation decline: Due to current taxation on all commodities and services, tremendous price hike is faced by citizens. Implementation of one-tax system and withdrawing all existing taxes on the citizens, will cause huge fall in the prices, thus inflation will have an end. Eventually, a new purchasing power will surface on which flourishing markets will emerge.

- Liberation from corruption: Due to nature of various taxes, the government structures the complex tax departments. Levying the wider range of taxes through various and complex structured taxation departments, corruption has become phenomenal. Tax evasion is the result of corruption in tax levying system. By abolishing all taxes on citizens through introducing one-tax system, corruption will bid farewell along with the outgoing tax regime.
- Expenditure reduction: Because of various taxes, the government structure several types of departments therefore a complex structure for taxation establishes, which require operational cost therefore increase system expenditures. A significant part of revenues is consumed to run these departments. Introduction of one-tax system will reduce system expenditure/ operational cost of the taxation departments, which will save a handsome amount in the exchequers.
- Introduction of one-tax system through abolishing all existing taxes on citizens, the existing tax department will not be required anymore.
- An end to account books: Because of various types of taxes, the Indian industry and commerce has to consume money, time and resources to maintain account books and other related documents for each tax out of wider range of taxation. It consumes tones of paper, printing ink and printers, and utilizes computer data management at par excellence. This consumes time, energy and money. And, finally these expenditures are included into the comedies/ production price, which are paid by the buyers. Replacement of existing tax system with the one-tax

system will ease investors and consumers through saving their time, energy and money.

- Profit Budget: India, these days, faces deficit budgets. Consequently, country's internal and foreign debt is increasing. By implementing one-tax system on property and wealth, the revenue will surge at higher scale. Hence, India will be able to zero its debts and at the same time the citizens will also get certain amount out of it as royalty – the monetary value of each person's equal right on natural resources.

- Freedom from food insecurity: After getting royalty from property and wealth tax revenue, food security will be ensured. It will end the means of income like beggary, sex labor, frauds, and other petty or organized crime. Besides, whatsoever forms of slavery that exist even today will cease to exist.

- Ending poverty and unemployment: Because of one-tax system poverty and unemployment will ultimately end though distribution of royalty among the citizens. At the same time, opportunities for human resources development and new investment, probably at lower scale but large in quantity will further the prosperity and economy.

- Emergence of new entrepreneur and proprietor: When the monetary benefits will trickle down to the poor and weaker sections of society, and thereby a new human capital with developed capacities and skills will surface, mostly youth will engage in trade, commerce and business rather than looking for the employment. This will further strengthen the economy and society.

- Decline in urban population pressure: The implementation of one-tax system will create an even economy in which cities, towns and villages will flourish economically. Therefore internal rural-urban migration will decline and cities will not face population pressure.

- Benefits to famers and laborers: Farmers, particularly peasant and small land holder, usually face scarcity of monetary resource; formal education; and technologies and instruments. This leg them behind in producing as well as proving services more through small quantity of labor and the time. They remain debt trapped. Usually, they sell their crops and other produces on lower price because they mostly are under debt of local money lenders or the financial institutions. Usually they don't have storage for crops and other produces to wait for better price. If one-tax system is implemented, through the royalty due to economic justice based one tax system, they will be able to get rid of debt, purchase modern instruments and provide better education to their children. On the same lines, other vulnerable sections and classes will also get rid of excessive labor as well as problems they face in their lives. They will become happy and live with self respect and without fear.

- Old age securities: A large number of elderly persons are unable to earn and depend on their children or other kin for their sustenance. Most of them face neglect and even humiliation from their own offspring and others. They have to live according to those whom they are dependent of. They are just *freedomless* persons. Despite their experience and desire, they are unable to play the role in society. After one-tax system, they will become self reliant.

They will have freedom, a role in society and live according to their desire.

- End to reservations and grants: Governments allocate funds, grants and ensure reservations for the weaker sections of society. This act is nothing but supplementing a tiny number of society since India's population has now exceeded 1.25 billion. Moreover reservations or subsidies are given for the electoral interest. Governments never realize they give a small quantity of funds through grants to the people as if it is a charity. Such practices create a row among the poor, vulnerable and underdeveloped. After one-tax system reservations and grants will not require. Their self respect will boost.

Calculation of dividend

The levied revenue through one-tax system can be called national income. The monetary share of the citizen in the national income, which popularly can be called royalty, formally should be called dividend. Its per capita amount will be according to total levied revenue through one-tax system, which may have rise and reduction. A part of it has to be 'dividend' among citizens without any difference and discrimination. It is essential to calculate people's and governments property. It can accurately be calculated only when the exact amount of the private property in the country is summed up and disclosed. Neither accurate record of private property exists, nor are governments willing to do that. According to law wealth details can be kept confidential therefore, it has to remain untold mystery. According to Indian media and experts estimates, per capita private property economic value is INR 80 trillion.

An estimated 73 percent of the wealth belongs to only 0.1 percent Indian rich. While implementing one-tax system, the levies on above the Line of Wealth can be called interest that one has to pay to the other citizens, which popularly can be said royalty because citizens are the owners of natural resources. In this regards, average rate of interest can be calculated 6 percent per annum although the actual interest rates in India on wealth and property mortgage is much higher.

CHAPTER 7

ONE-TAX SYSTEM, NATIONAL INCOME AND ECONOMIC EQUALITY

Total private wealth India is worth INR 800 trillion. Meanwhile, the country's wealthy persons are over 0.1 percent. They simply possess 73 percent of the country's total private property. If minimum estimates about the economic value of the above line of wealth property are to be calculated, 70 percent of the property will be multiplied with the 800 trillion. 800 x 70 = 560,000 INR trillion.

In a bid to simplify the net government revenues and citizens' royalty through an example, the possession above the Line of Wealth if annually taxed in India through 5 percent interest rate on the value of wealth, the annual tax collection will be INR 560,000 x 5 subtracted by 100 = INR 280,00 trillion. This we can call annual national income. India's average annual budget is 4,5000 trillion. After deducting government expenditure out of the annual tax collection, the remaining amount will be INR 235,000 (INR 280,000 – INR 450,00 = INR 235,000) trillion. These INR 235,000 trillion will be net annual surplus revenues that can be called surplus national income. India's population is 1.25 billion. If each citizen of India is given INR 10,000 monthly out of surplus national income, this will amount: 1.25 billion persons x INR 10,000 x 12 months = INR 1500 trillion.

Therefore, the citizens received ten thousand rupees royalty every month; the total royalty or dividend from the national surplus will be 150 trillion. The remaining surplus national income will be INR 1350 trillion per annum, and will be part of the government treasury, which can be used to further develop India, meet the further import requirements and make the country debt free.

None will have extreme adverse impacts across the citizenry. Everyone will be prosperous and happy. Income will not be scares. Nothing will scare. It will be an end to the existing exploitation and oppression. Harmony in the society will replace antagonism. The new centers of knowledge will be established, wisdom will flourish, the governance will be easier as this will also evade various forms of the crime, and hence it will remain focused on implementation of law and delivering justice. Malpractices will reduce to greater extent, paving way for the forces of positivity. The distance between the governments and the citizens will reduce. All forms of social leadership will keep cohesive.

CHAPTER 8

WEALTH, FAMILY AND THE STATE

An ideal economy can be built by implementing one tax system levied on more than line of wealth, the revenue generated out of which can be called national income. By doing so, the all other kinds of taxes on the citizens will be abolished; furthermore, a share from national income will be distributed equally among the citizens as dividend. Because of this, the government expenditure will also reduce. Indian economy today is complex, self-contradictory, costly, impractical, unscientific, unjust and low yielding in the context of income as well as revenue. It also require broader infrastructure. Inversely, the new economy based on one-tax system that will generate national income will be very simple, lethargy free, open, rational, cost efficient, and yielding greater in the context of income and revenues. In a bid to establish such a new economy, we have to reform legal regime as well as administrative framework like:

Elimination of confidentiality and un-disclosure of private property details:

A law of privacy for the wealth in the country due to which citizens cannot get information on anyone's private wealth and associated tax details. This is against dignity of citizens, transparency, freedom and democracy.

A few citizens of the country own most of country's wealth, while the government acts only as their representative, in that case government's facilitation to the wealthy for their asset's confidentiality is being party to a few against overwhelming majority. This can happen only in a colony, not in an independent and free country. Such a black law is an unjust, unjustified and an insult for the citizens. Because of such a law, the citizenry is being looted by the rulers, wealthy and bureaucracy. It provides, in fact, the shelter and protection to the economic, financial, and monetary criminals and wealth mafia. This results into income tax payments and returns discrepancies for the wealthy whose actual assets and taxation has been made confidential legally. Ultimately, revenues of the country remain lower than that of what actually should be. This also results into black money or in other words un-acknowledged and untaxed money. If the law for the confidentiality of wealth and taxation is abolished, people of the country will give their popular verdict against the excessive wealth accumulators.

Under the guise of this law of confidentiality, all industrialists, business hegemonies, administrators and statuesque intellectuals do commit act of economic wrongdoing by paying lesser taxes and filling income tax returns. Besides wealthy, the constitutional and public post holders like the President, Prime Minister,

Lok Sabha Speaker (Chief whip of the Parliament's lower house) and Chief Justice of the Supreme Court are deceiving the society by being silent on the matter. The lack law of wealth and tax details confidentiality is a cover to hide the economic and fiscal malpractices and theft by the wealthy.

Law of right assessment of property:

The property valuation law in the country is irrational. It, like the law of confidentiality for property, wealth and tax details, plays a major role in the increase of black money. Because of this, property worth millions is fraudulently valued in the hundreds of thousands for tax evasion. This situation has created three pronged taxation issues – registry of property in the land record; property resell collector rate on the ownership transfer of the property; and the real value of property at market rate. Revenues through registry of the property in urban hubs is hundreds times lower than what actually they should be. The resell collector rate is levied when a property undergoes the registry process mostly due to resell. If the property is unsold, it contains government-assessed value according to the registry. Thus, it cause decline in the resell collector tax revenues, in the meantime it is sold on market rate that use to be higher than the property value assessed by the government agency (however the sell and purchase transaction is kept hidden). Mostly property owners decrease the worth of the property in the documents to evade sell or taxes. Resultantly, the official record of the land valuation in India is inaccurate and wrong. The market value of property is not surveyed therefore government data in this case is unreliable.

Line of Wealth and the Average Wealth:

Every citizen in the country has right to own wealth unlimited extent. It needs to be changed. Wealth rights will have to be divided into two parts: (i) fundamental rights, and (ii) acquired or legal rights. The wealth in fundamental wealth rights should not be taxed, and it should have an average ceiling for all the citizens. Meanwhile, the wealth in the category of acquired or legal wealth rights shall have to be taxed since it is the one that crosses the ceiling for the private wealth holding – the Line of Wealth. Therefore, the owner has to pay tax as a royalty to the citizens for holding excessive property at the prevailing interest rate. And, the owner of that property should be considered the one who is indebted to the society.

Compulsory registration of a family:

Families in the country should be registered. Legislation should be done in this regards. A representative, the lead, of a family unit should be selected with consensus of all family members for the purpose of government, society al and family related engagements. There should be no limitations on the number of family members by anyone. Unlike the secotral and religion based family or personal law, for example Muslim and Hindu family laws in India, all family members, without gender discrimination, will have equal rights on all movable, immovable and monetary assets of the parents. Family members will have right to exclude anyone amongst them from the family or include else one, provided that inheritance economic justice is made and parents as well as older or elders are taken well care of. If a new person is included into the family, he or she be conferred equal right in either inheritance of family elders provided that the members of the family are agree to make someone part of the family.

Process of implementation:

- The consensually selected representative of the family will have to give all details about the family members' name, gender, age and related data, identity and similar documents as well as quantity and the details of wealth along with the value of the property on the time of purchase. A person should be completely free to evaluate its assets, without interference of the State.
- The representative of the family and/or adult members should submit the details duly signed by them in front of the concerned authority. The ceiling of the wealth possession and tax on it will be announced based on the recommendation by a commission appointed by the government or the State; however, the details should be made public. The recommendations that are made public will be final.
- The wealth rights of citizen will be fundamental and for individuals, whether they are members of a family or not. The tax on the wealth exceeding line of wealth will be levied on individual basis.
- Providing wrong details to the concerned authority will be considered fraud and punishable offense.
- Family details will be categorized as public record, not the confidential in anyway. A citizen will be given unalienable right to obtain these details of other.

- A property has to be sold through open bid by following a simple but open procedure of the bidding.
- If there is more than one buyer of a property, it will be sold to the one who bids highest. The highest bid will be considered as an actual market value of that asset.
- The tax and other procedures will not imply on those whose property sell is below 20 percent of market value compared with the purchase/original rate of the property, besides the seller being bellow the line of wealth.
- The provision for mandatory transfer of property will apply equally to all types of private property.
- The post wealth rights and tax ratio, once the announcement of the market value of a property is made, the representative of a family based on the number of his family members, will calculate the tax on the assets shown in his statement. If the property is not bellow line of wealth, one will have to submit notice with the concerned government department. If the value of the property increases in the resale of the property, again it has to undergo the process whether the resale value of property is above or below the line of wealth.
- If the property tax on the taxable property is not paid in the prescribed limits, the state will sale whole or a part of the property through an open bid to the persons who bids the highest. After deducting the property tax, the remaining amount will be handed over to the owner of that property.
- Members of a family collectively will also be able to get a property of high value after making a mutual consent. And, their fundamental rights will stand

valid provided that a consent affidavit is made for collective purchase.

- Out of total revenues through wealth tax from citizens, the government can separate the amount required for the country's budget. The total revenues out of wealth tax on the wealth above the line of wealth will be considered as the national income generated from natural resources and rest of the economy. All details of the national income have to be for public domain. A citizen will be entitled to demand and hence receive a true certified copy of it

- An amount out of total national income should also be allocated for emergencies. The amount for emergencies will be maintained. Besides, the previous dues on the government can also be deducted from the national income gradually or fully according to as well as in the better interests of the country. And, the remaining amount will be deposited directly into bank accounts of all citizens equally. The government will have no right to cut a citizen's amounts in lieu of any kind or service.

- The amount spent on national security could be kept confidential with consent of president, cabinet and top brass of army for a particular period of maximum three years. After the proscribed period, the details of such expenditure should be made public, which in fact should not be kept hidden from the people of the country on any pretext.

- If a property is of high worth, but does not attract buyers or the would-be-buyers or the sale value decline of the property occurs, government should consider purchasing it on actual value.

If the one-tax system elaborated earlier is compared to the present tax system, the new system is extremely simple, short, less expensive, real, transparent, logical, scientific, progressive and justifiable. This system will establish a complete balance between production, exchange, distribution and consumption. It will provide justice and protection to every person.

It will provide competent individual independence and opportunity. It will ensure sustainable utilization of natural resources. Greed to accumulate wealth will be discouraged. All the productive means of the country will sustainably be utilized. Besides, the surplus revenue if any apart from described above cannot be kept unproductive. By this, the country and the citizens will be prosperous. Freedom and equality will be outcomes. A healthful, happy and satisfied people would be the climax result of this.

It will eradicate bias, discriminations and differences based on the communal, caste, sectarian, ethnic, regional, gender, business, trade, commerce and economic as well as other types of difference from the country. A harmonious society with mutual trust and cooperation will flourish along with the characteristics of generosity, humanity, renunciation, morality, duty and naturalism, and compassion.

An enlightened citizenry will be the nation. Free from food, shelter and cloth insecurity and happy they will be. Thus, the real mirage and secret of a true life would be unfolded.

CHAPTER 9

A FREE WORLD

Important will be the impacts of economic justice based fiscal regime on the world. World is a global villages since last a couple of decades. Communication revolution in the electronics, computation, artificial intelligence, virtual connectivity, mobile telephony, faster plains, bullet trains, and steady ships, rail and road transportation has just interwoven world into a swift accessibility of people and goods. Business, industry, excursion and market are no more a domestic affair. It is world affair, now. Mingling the drops from various cultures and becoming an ocean of diversity and multi-cultural setting is phenomenal in almost whole of the world through interchange of traditions, beliefs, norms, family bonds, wearing, art, design, fashion, entertainment, knowledge, education, and information. The globalization of trade and commerce has turned previously country-bound citizens into the global citizenry. Immigration and choosing a nation and a country for oneself is the climax of human face. No doubt, these are the embryos of a new world that has to occur after certain decades.

On the same lines meanwhile, there exists globalization of crime and terrorism in the both syndical and non-syndical means. This in certain cases is backed by the governments of various countries. Besides, the new deadly weapons have also replaced old. No doubt world has joined the race of more deadly weaponry. Effective international governance does not exist. Use of might to exploit as well as suppress each other by the governments is the world polity. In their selfish interests, mighty countries are trying to keep weaker ones under-educated and lesser-skilled. Confronting countries interfere into each other's internal affairs and cause political turmoil.

In the name of creating a world trade and economy, minimal government in economy is demanded. World trade or industry is an excuse to attain the interests of the powerful. They proudly take advantage of the world that is not developed. When these soft means of the world exploitation fail, use of weapons and military might is resorted. Amid this, the intervention of businessmen tycoons in the world's politics has further pushed backward the world poor. They make effort the takeover of country-rule by their business-supporters in the different parts of the world. Wealthy businesspersons are helping politician of their choice to capture the power, where possible. Once done, these tycoons compel them to favor in their business interests against the norms and justice. If their goals are not achieved, they attempt to replace such governments. Governments mostly bow in front of these business interests in the form of policies directly or indirectly associated with the trade, commerce, and industry. They are not made accountable and they do not contribute for humanity. They want to become further wealthy. They cause terrible consequences due to that. World people have suffered and express dissent against it.

Scientific advancements are the reason of large scale production. Meanwhile, poverty, unemployment, hunger, crime, dissatisfaction and unrest have also grown at large scale. Economic inequality today has caused cross-borders movements and uprisings.

The wealthy is becoming wealthier every day, and poor becomes poorer. Public dissatisfaction is causing rebel as well. In India, for example this has been airing the *Naxalite* violence and elsewhere this has exhibited various forms of terrorism. Unimaginably, governments despite forming prop-people policies, further add to the dissatisfaction of people. The common man is horrified, and stuck in the blind alley. In the final result, it is economic injustice that has caused such kind of public insecurity and dissatisfaction.

An issue today between two countries, is an issue between two people as well. Civil unrest is everywhere. Class antagonism is also a reality of today like past. Food insecurity and conflicts due to that are becoming a world phenomenon. Economic justice and equality, the necessities for the essential democracy, is the only way forward. This and this alone, can lead the world to a peaceful transformation. Economic justice vision is potent to gain popular support. It will prevent conflict, strife and unrest, bring about peace and realize democratic rights. A free society is possible. A free world indeed!

CHAPTER 10

ON SOCIAL DISORDER

Today society is victim of many kinds of disruptions. The current social system is neither able to check disturbance nor it is able to organize the society.

Strife over sect, caste, territory, language, gender, occupation, age-group, color, education, urban, rural, rich and poor are destroying the society. In violence this has caused inter-people distances, deaths and loss of property of many. Tragedy. The constant fear and panic due to conflicts have impacted psych-composite of the people.

In fact, a social order is the comprehensive agreement as well as arrangement among the people or peoples to provide level playing field for the diverse interests and rest all. In a bid to maintain social order, societies have developed laws, traditions, beliefs and taboos. Such a social arrangement through polity is also to ensure fundamental human rights of everyone.

LINE OF WEALTH

The main reason behind the conflicts among people is economy, essentially based on the consumption. Consumption and in all of its connotations in origin are produced out of natural resources. Therefore, the natural resources are the wealth as such. Everyone desires to control maximum wealth for the ongoing as well as future requirements. Since natural resources are scarce, the shortcoming is the arbitrary accumulation of wealth. This is the-root cause of antagonism in the society.

Justice is the only resolution to the conflicts, strife and antagonism. The existing system does not offer justice. Though, every country has laws to provide justice but they have failed to provide real justice to the citizenry, simply because the systems are not committed to provide justice as such. Therefore, every now and then when pro-people governments rule, they make the new laws and amend the existing ones. Since formation of governments is fundamental based on to take over the power therefore power-mongering has become central point of electoral democracy rather than justice as such, hence the essence of democracy and governance has dissipated.

According to existing practices in the world, everyone is free to earn on the basis of merit, interests, and competence, and at the same time one is free to utilize and save earnings. Savings are the wealth. When income is more than expenditure, gaining property and thereafter accumulation of wealth happens. Income, if earned through one's labor, is based a vast range of factor including mental and physical abilities. Persons are different from each other due to their characteristics. And, the gains are by those who utilize their specialized characteristics fully and freely if opportune. This is also one of the reasons for gradual possession of the natural resources by a few. Nothing is left for weaker or poor for the consumption. Only trend of might is right does exist, justice does not. A rule of jungle indeed!

Neither freedom. Nor Justice. A hollow justice and shell of freedom are exhibited. Freedom can never be one or a few persons', freedom is when it is for all. A freedom without its legitimate boundaries cannot can only ensure the freedom of others. The boundary-less freedom cause arrogance and contributes to the accumulation of wealth. A person has boundary-less freedom to poses assets. No limitations to such freedom are there. It is nothing but independence to poses unlimited property. Finally, the wealthy are arrogant, and exploit the wreathless. Powerful has control over most of the natural resources and the weaker, the poor depends on them both in terms of production and consumption. One has to, because of this, do anything to survive. Rebels thus happen to get rid of the phenomena.

Because of the similar interests, society is under continuous process of grouping, re-grouping and fragmentation. Basically these groups are formed to avoid injustice and tyranny of powerful. Being organized together increases their power so that they try to get rid of their slavery. But their purpose is not to establish justice. On the basis of their interests, different types of groups are formed in the society. Since their interests are contrary to each other, therefore, it is natural to have differences, disputes, and quarrels among them. This hampers the unity of the people, the society gets disintegrated. The world today is an open theatre of that. Every moment weaker, marginalized and poor become is made victim by the powerful. Such oppression and victimization lead them to join the groups of their common interest. Basically, it is insecurity of the weaker, marginalized and poor that has caused their group formation with the outcome of social movements for change. Mostly they popularly create movement; however some time the movements become violent. Today, numerous social groups are active around the issues and matters related to the language, gender, sect, region, employment and age-aspect. They do all with reference to the social order. Majority is either victim or left behind in the context of development and socio-economic justice. Irony that leadership of such activism is mostly affluent persons that claims to be the vanguard poor, marginalized and victimized. There have been many examples that indicate their selfish interests. Social groups require resources for activism, and the affluent leaderships can afford that. Due to this, the opinion and decisions of such affluent leadership of the weaker and poor are imposed on the activists. This is the reason behind one-person leadership phenomena of various social movements.

Such leadership in many cases has no vision about the social justice. They just have activism within certain ring, thus monotony and stereo-type in social movements grow. Certain among such activism including ethnicity, territory, and communalism also pose serious threat to the society because of their orthodox, misleading or self-centric approach. A justice is also required within the social movements. Therefore, until a just society is not created, such *groupism* will not cease to exist. A cohesive and harmonious society is only possible thereafter.

CHAPTER 11

PURPOSE OF ECONOMY AND IMPORTANCE OF JUSTICE

The fundamental purpose of the economy is to provide consumables in abundances to meet consumption requirement and avert scarcity of consumables. The natural resources are the real economic sources that are processed into consumables for human use. This requires a lot of efforts both physically and mentally. The scientific development hitherto has also created various specializations in a bid to have produce. Therefore, the industrial process and manufacturing as well as services today cannot be delivered by one person only.

In a bid to avoid scarcity, human has developed science, art, structure and process of economy. Besides, consumables are produced by a group of persons specialized in various skills. Therefore their production is large, and scarcity of consumables today does not happen usually. Similarly, the rest producer or manufacturers produce or manufacture commodities or consumable in a large amount. The quantity of such a production by various groups of manufacturers and service providers is exchanged when seen at the household level, and this process can be called an exchange. Definitely, market is the places for this grand exchange. Exchange, hence, is a vital link in development of the economic system.

The diversified skills combined in a group form to produce consumables have reduced per capita labor on the production. To avoid large volume of manufacturing and production cost of the consumables, there have emerged the industrial, agricultural and services hubs as well as heavy industrial complexes. Moreover, a production more than the demand, if, when, and where happened, has declined the demand of the consumables in the market, therefore caused decline in their prices.

Human has made enormous progress by continuously improving the processes of production and exchange to the extent that the labor has reduced in the process of production.

Meanwhile, technologies have been introduced in the process of production to reduce human labor for the production, while on the other hand market has been made focus for exchange to the production in lieu of money. The monitory, banking and financial systems are also important pillars of the economy. Advancements in robotics and artificial intelligence, has also reduced the consumption of energy for the production. Due to this, lifestyle has changed.

In the developing world, heavy industrial complexes have caused shut-down of small industries mostly involving greater human labor. Therefore, demand for human labor has decreased, and the volume of production has increased. Besides, due heavy industrial complexes, the demand of natural resources for the production of consumables has also increased.

Similarly, the demand of human labor in the market process has also decreased to certain extent. Modern technologies have taken over the various forms of human labor in terms for communication, transportation etc. Production and market both are now global. Therefore, the manufacturing of the modern technological devices has also become at larger scale. Human today have succeeded to get production through smaller human labor, which is bound to create crises in social system. Unemployment has increased mostly due to this, and a new poor is the outcome which is insecure and vulnerable. Meanwhile, the investors have become more wealthy and powerful. The accumulation of wealth has further increased causing larger economic inequality. The discontent, strife and antagonism are intensified and are bound to lead us all to the various kinds of violence.

Contrary to the fundamentals of a cross-sectional social order, the possession and control of production and market by a few has resulted into unjust distribution of the benefits in the society which is based on technological developments, production and market. Therefore, the additional income earned from modern production and market, needs to be distributed among the society for economic justice. This alone can be said a fair economic system.

LINE OF WEALTH

The decrease in the purchase power due to increase in the quantity and vulnerability of poor, and increase in the cost of the modern industrial complex and the market, has reduced the demand vis-à-vis total volume of the production in the world. A severe economic inequality has got birth resultantly. Besides, due to modernization of industry and market, the demand of capital in the economy has increased.

Czerny is the sole owner of the natural resources in a country therefore the rich has also right on the additional income that results from these resources. The additional income should be divided equally among the citizenry through the calculation based on the resources with reference to the production. Besides, the very much machinery or technical devices themselves are created out of as well as through the process of natural resources, therefore people have also the right on them as well, therefore this factor should also be considered as a context or the part of the income distribution among the society. The income only earned from the labor should be a person's sole ownership. Besides, the private wealth of all kind, including the complexes industry, when crosses the line of wealth, should be shared among all in a country, and be practically forwarded to them through taxation which is one-tax system. Such taxation should be considered a royalty of the people, and may be called share of a citizen in the natural resources and the structure to process natural resources for the production of consumables. It can also be called dividend in the national income. The contemporary economic system is juxtaposed to such economic justice mechanism.

Example, a country is a huge company and it has the equal share in capital by all the citizens. Therefore, as company after deducting the expenditures, it distributes the net profit proportionate to the number of shareholders. Similarly, after taxing the wealth accumulator on the formula of line of wealth, as expressed in earlier paragraph, the revenue would be national income, which has to be distributed among all citizens proportionately hence called dividend here.

This distribution can also be understood by another simple example. Let's assume that there is a mango tree and it has more than 1000 mangoes. The total number of people is 100 and all those people have equal rights on the mangos. On the basis of justice, everyone will have right on 10 mangoes. But in order to use them, they will have to get the mangoes first. It will require hard work, intellect and capability. Since, capabilities of all people are neither equal nor the same. If freedom to take mangoes is given, and equal right on the mangoes are forgotten, the more capable, sturdy and healthy will take more mangoes, meanwhile weaker rest will take less or probably no mango. Therefore, freedom to have control of natural resources and associated things without ensuring rights, create accumulation of wealth, and majority will become poorer, profitless or benefit-less. A fair and prudent solution is those with more capability or might should be allowed to get more than 10 mangoes. However, possession of more than 10 mangoes should be divided into two parts like in sharecropping between the landlord and the toiler. In this, the owner of the land gets one part of the production as share of ownership, while other part is right of earned labor by the toiler. Assume that the capable persons get only the share of their utilized labor, meanwhile the share of ownership above the certain line of wealth goes to the society; both will remain peaceful and cohesive, turning socio-economic antagonism into harmony. Besides, the weaker, marginalized and poor will also not face scarcity resources for purchase. Hence a news society will develop free from antagonism, along with the flourishing harmony, faith, cooperation, spirituality, renunciation and human relations. All will complement each other. It will ensure the socio-economic security for all in the real and practical sense. It will be impossible without justice for all.

CHAPTER 12

EXPLOITATION FREE MARKET SYSTEM

Market is a place for sell and purchases of commodities/consumables by producer or seller and the consumer. There is also a third stratum in the market called merchants, shopkeepers, intermediaries and hawker. They buy goods from producer or their suppliers, store and sell to the buyers that include consumers, traders, businesspersons, and retailers.

They profit from sales. They are well acquainted with the information and knowledge of their business. They buy the commodities/consumables cheaper and sell at higher price. They also usually profit, exceptionally however they have loss.

The prices of commodities fluctuate depending on the demand and supply in the market. It is human nature that every person desires to sell their production at maximum price, and wants to buy the things at the minimum price. Therefore, the value of any item in the market is not fundamentally related to the labor involved in its production. On the basis of demand and sell, the independent market decides the prices of the commodities.

Demand and supply in the market is not always stable but keeps changing. When the demand for something is more and the supply is less, then the value or price of that item increases, vice versa prices decreases. This causes hoarding when traders stock the commodities when their price is lower, and sell only when their prices are higher.

In fact, the price of commodities should be fixed on the basis of labor utilized for their production. From the point of view of the market, the price of any item in the market should be fixed on the basis of labor utilized in its production however this not possible practically. Only demand and supply are the price determining factors. Other factors do also exist. The cost of production has different aspects. Therefore, those whose production cost is lower they earn profit by selling their produce at less price, whereas when the production cost is high, the producers have to bear the loss. But the market does not have anything to do with it. It keeps doing its job as a weird machine. When there is a huge gap in demand and supply situation, there is a huge fluctuation in the market rate of related items. Many people take high profit from this, others suffer heavy losses. For some people this may be big thing, but it is a normal practice for the markets.

Market is a place of competition over sale and purchase of production. High prices are the desires of the sellers but the fear of competitors does exist. Mostly buyers compare prices at different shops and venders, and then purchase at whatsoever lower price of products is available in the market. Those venders who sale at higher prices get lower profit provided that the number of buyers is not according to their expectations.

The fluctuation in prices due to demand and supply cannot be called wrong, besides artificial price hike due to hoarding is also an existing phenomena. This creates an unfair and exploitative market, which finally adversely impacts the buyers. Hoarders often gains high profits and seldom losses.

In market, the purchase due to urgencies cost the buyer a lot. They usually are on the weaker sections of society so far the market mechanism is concerned. Sometime such urgency is due to time period of usability of a product. Such sellers also earn losses. This is another vicious cycle that adversely impact such sellers and buyers both.

Although governments in various countries including India have made laws to curb this practice; however the wealthy market-exploiters prevent the law, only a few are nabbed. An end to this can only be the market planning and development along with legal framework and watch-dogs based on Line of Wealth. By this, none will receive negative impacts of hoarding and similar practices in the market, nor will have the loss due to exploitive means of lowering the prices of producers. A hoarding and market manipulation penalty, heavy in volume, should be imposed to curb such practices through proper complaint and watchdog mechanism based on the law.

Exploitation free market system does not mean elimination of open market. It is just to curb market manipulation practices. In this regard, a public education process should also be initiated. The market should be free; however alternative measures should be taken to curb inappropriate tendencies. Another solution to the hoarding and similar practices is the purchase of hoarding prone comedies by the prospective governments and their sale on appropriate prices in the market.

FAIR ECONOMY: A REVIEW OF EXISTING IDEOLOGIES

Although the basic purpose of the economy is to bring prosperity in society, but the importance of economic justice cannot be ignored. Justice in the context of economy means prosperity through natural resources income by their fair distribution among all.

Two ideologies are notable regarding economy with reference to people: Capitalism and Marxism. No theory does exist for the rural economy per se. Capitalism and Marxism cannot coexist.

The instinct of a society is to prefer fair economic system; however certain forces resist fair economies due to their interests, which can only be served in a particular economic system. These forces are economically and politically strong therefore they use their power to create illusions and propagate to hinder any possible alternative and the very much ideology for that. To attain this, they harm livelihood of those who promote possible new system. They terrorize, lure and assassin those who strive for better ideology for the society. Ultimately, truth will prevail!

Capitalism can be considered as a self-developed ideology as it perfectly matches industrial human psyche. Basically every person is interest oriented or selfish, and due to such human nature, one adopts the simplest path to fulfill his selfish interests. He or she wants to keep the life safe, convenient and happy. Even a trend of competition for that exists strongly. A person applies intellect, physical, mental and all other abilities to bypass others. Everyone wants to establish his or her right on more wealth to meet his present and protect future. For the sake of this interest, one takes advantage of others' less competence, ignorance, weakness and needs.

To a greater extent, capitalism believes in human nature and even accepts it. Capitalism, so far as its doctrine is concerned, does not include direct exploitation, usurpation, and power grab however it includes accumulation of wealth to the unlimited extent for which it justifies itself on the basis competence. In capitalism an individual is free to earn, spend and save earned resources to unlimited extent. Accumulation of private wealth to unlimited extent is not a wrong act in capitalism. Capitalism terms it individual liberty. Liberalism, the refined form of capitalism, has also same approach to the global extent. A system based on capitalism accepts no obstruction to this individual liberty. According to capitalism, a person can choose any kind of industry, trade or service to gain maximum profit using his or her intellectual, physical and financial resources; besides he or she can also determine the value or price of his or her production and services. At the same time, he or she is responsible for the profit or loss in the business.

Ideologically capitalism believes in complete freedom of individual in all aspects. It professes and create agency for competition to earn wealth to unlimited extent. New inventions and technological developments happen around, which further kicks off the competition and upscale the market economy that is based on greater produce with elevated quality. The enhanced quantity of the production and services also lowers the prices.

Capitalism to certain extent accepts the right of ownership on natural resources. Theoretically, however, it does not recognize the equal ownership of all on the natural resources. It does not accept ceiling on natural resources ownership. Therefore, it completely rejects this idea of the fundamental right of all citizens on the natural resources in various manifestations. The gospel of capitalism is more and more freedom to a person, prohibition of any sort is unfair. Such kind of unlimited freedom cannot be justified.

On the basis of justice, freedom means an equal freedom to all. A maximum amount of freedom in fact can be provided to each. Therefore, there must be median limits to freedom. The axioms of an optimum limit or an average limit of freedom is a matter of further discussion. Unlimited freedom is nothing but arrogance. Justifying a system based on arrogance is ignorance. The outcome of this ignorant, unjust and inaccurate recognition of capitalism is clearly visible in the society where huge economic inequality is phenomenal. In this system a handful of persons establish monopoly on the natural resources, power and property, meanwhile the remaining others, the largest section of society, suffers due dispossession and misery. The very much concept of capitalism, and the laws based on similar notions make an environment of non-transcending social process. It is just a denial of justice to all.

Marxism, on the other hand, is a reaction to injustice originated in capitalism; however its fundamentals are based on equality. It rejects right of private property. Simply it doctrines that the poor alone have right on all natural resources, and the governments are nothing but the representation of that right. Therefore, socialist practices, based on the theories of Marxism, give possession of the entire property, resources, and other forms of assets of a country solely to the State. Thus, the State carries all activities like production, exchange, distribution and consumption management. In this system, open market does not exist. It is the State that determines the value, or price of everything. Individual liberties and private property are non-existent. The State apparatus has remained solely responsible for providing employment, deciding payouts (whether in kind or cash), providing food, cloths, house, education, health facilities and other similar human needs to citizenry. Everyone received his required things in accordance to rules made by government. All used to be provided the consumables equally. It did not discriminate or elevated persons on the basis of qualifications, abilities, skills or the labor. Though there was equality in this system but it does not gave freedom to human persons. It has caused social monotony and stereotype. Due to the control over all the means of production, and in the absence of popular and transparent procedure of personnel appointment, only politically associated persons used get influential positions. Efficacy and efficiency were neglected. People did not felt inclined to work hard. They worked to appease the government to escape any wrath. Since means of productions were not properly managed, the production reduced. And, in the absence of freedom, persons became machines.

The dark side of socialist system is the housing of economic and political rights within the power corridor. Power turns persons totalitarian therefore they do not tolerate ideological dissent. There remains power instability as well. In order to keep control over power, opponents are dealt as enemies. Thus, game of power and conspiracies begins. The loyal of ruling political party remain safe. Social welfare becomes irrelevant. Government sees every person with suspicion. They monitor each and every activity of the citizens, which results distrust among the people. And, they just do not speak freely. Nobody knows who among them is a spy of the system and informing about their activities to the government. This ends the freedom of speech and thought. Skills and capability becomes rare. Finally, economy collapses and the country suffers.

Due to the reasons shared earlier in this chapter, both ideologies do not create a composite society. Capitalist economy cause huge production but lacks proper distribution and does not tender the income from economic growth to the commoner. Freedom is meaningless in capitalism and commoners are pushed towards extreme poverty that is akin to slavery.

A commoner, in socialist system, on the other hand faces similar situation. In this system, production reduces and the commoner has to face the misery of poverty. If compared, capitalism is comparatively lesser troublesome for society than that of hitherto practiced socialist system. Capitalism, although, has meaningless freedom, freedom of speech does exist. The forces grown out of and based on power and accumulation of wealth appear differently however they one in the same thing. A capitalist society doesn't control individuals in direct terms in comparison with the practices of communist regime. Due to these reasons, capitalism defeated the socialist system based on Marxism. This does not justify capitalism. Had capitalism provided justice to people, Marxism would not have been born. Hence, the end of Marxist communist-regime state system is not important, significant is its birth. Although human society today does not have powerful alternatives to the capitalism, yet Marxism has given alternatives. Marxism has given a new thinking to the society to march forward. Therefore, Marxism should be considered a milestone in search of a fair order.

Important question is why both ideologies have failed to establish justice in society? Commonly it is replied that the failure of Capitalism and Marxism is inherent in the human tendency of unfairness. It is a superficial reply. The actual reply to the question is both do not qualify properly the test for justice. We must know this that a minor deviation with justice in any philosophy or theory can cause unexpected results. More tragic and unpleasant, indeed. Marxism is an example of this.

Ideological drawbacks of capitalism are the limelight freedom with *undercast* equality. It ignores real equality.

A real equality is a natural right born along with a baby. It cannot be seen in the perspective of ability, power and any other specialty. Therefore we require thinking for the weaker and poor and redefining the unalienable basic rights that a competent as well as powerful may not violate. Simultaneously, freedom of a person is not defined as yet. Talent is not something because of which justice may be denied or one is given ultimate freedom and absolute rights. Looking with the glasses of ability and power will infringe the freedom of people and make them slaves. Besides, no one's right can be determined on basis of his or her talent. Unfortunately this happens. It is unjust, indeed. The phenomena create confrontation and injustice that will lead horrible ends. Instead of awakening the conscience of the person, such happenings disallow people to resist their greed and selfishness. No system can be established on these foundations. Therefore, expecting peace, security, satisfaction and prosperity in such scenario would be wrong.

Similarly, practiced socialist system based on Marxism remained unjust, full of flaw and principle-free. It absolutely denied the right to hold private property, which negates basic human freedom. It also eliminates the original motivation of the person to develop himself and his persona. Equality without freedom has no meaning. It is a kind of slavery in its own way. No society or a person can accept it. It is fundamentally against human psyche.

The communist countries' system did not distinguish between society and the State. State takeover of the property and all means of production due the notion that everything belongs to the people and thereby to the state is a diktat to the society and act to create slaves by power. Therefore, no agency was left to curb *powerism* and totalitarianism. A small group of people accumulated the power, shared it with each other, took over the resources and had luxurious lives in the communist countries. The remaining others were powerless and underwent miseries. Therefore, instead of becoming a classless society based on equality, there were ruling class and the ruled ones.

The third major drawback of Marxist ideology is the concept of class struggle. The existence of such a permanent class struggle has never existed in human society. The creation of classes in the society arises due to the conflict interests. The real reason for this collision is lack of justice in the system. Due to which every person gets threatened by the powerful. Therefore, the threatened one refuges in any social group to protect himself or herself. He or she selects the social group in accordance with the nature of threat and the circumstances arise out of that particular situation. Often, one changes group when situation changes. Similarly, if there are multiple threats, one joins various social groups at the same time. In its origin, it is not a struggle among or between the groups but it is a struggle for individuals. Everyone wants more prosperity and independence then the rest. Therefore, whatever one does, it is to fulfill selfish interests and for that matter one does not even hesitate to do injustice to the others. If one becomes comparatively powerful, one's thoughts and patterns of thinking change. And for him the meaning of justice and injustice also changes. The person argues on the basis of his or her own selfish interests. Therefore, he or she in accordance to current interests even joins the groups whom he opposed yesterday. If the idea of class struggle is right, even after change in social orders, no person would change their class loyalty. This also reflects from the double-slandered characteristics of leaders who believe in the class struggle. Therefore, the reality of class struggle is a deception. The power of the workers is also a bluff, which is an important part of Marxist ideology. Similarly, the Marxist concept of surpluses value is also totally wrong.

The economic justice vision is free from incomplete and flawed beliefs in Marxism and Capitalism. It is based on complete and natural justice. It is a prudent coordination of freedom and equality. It critically review the maximum authority of the most qualified person and the minimum right of the weak person simultaneously. It respects ability as well as accepts birthrights (natural rights) of a person too. It neither profess unlimited private wealth rights nor does it invalidate the wealth right. It is a middle path to balance the powerful and the weak, thus it can be acceptable to both.

The economic justice vision neither ignores nor neglect fundamentals of social justice. It strives for a fair distribution of surplus revenue through national income generated through one-tax system as elaborated with details in previous chapters. It makes a clear distinction between the existence and rights of both society and the power. It recognizes power on one hand, while on the other it also recognizes the supremacy of society over power. Instead of making power as a chieftain or regulating authority of society, it only recognizes responsibility of power or system for protection. This vision provides maximum equal freedom to all citizens. It does not recognize authority of power to make biased laws, instead it profess the legislation based on justice.

In this regards, it pursues scientific, logical, fair and transparent path of fundamental right of every citizen as detailed in previous chapters. It believes every citizen has right to natural resources and wealth in their direct and indirect manifestations; at the same time it connects these rights with collective prosperity to end poverty. It recognizes only the social justice for economic disparity; however it also envisions the alternate means to equate this disparity. It interprets the wealth rights that are uncontroversial as well as can be acceptable to all. This vision gives every person the complete opportunity to develop their abilities and choose the fields of their interests. Besides, it advocates complete independence and support to the people in achieving their goal. It eliminates the dispute, complexity and conspiracies regarding the wealth right. It is simple and transparent. It talks about the noncontroversial private wealth right that can be acceptable to all sections of the society. If any exception arises regarding private wealth rights, the economic justice vision believes in fairness as well as comprehensive and essential justice to address that matter.

The economic justice vision does not divide society on the lines of caste, religion, gender, profession, age, race or color etc. it doesn't believe in exclusive rights to anyone. It neither professes reservation or grants nor does it believes in discrimination on the basis of minority or majority. Instead it believes in equal rights to all citizens including the equal right to protection. It advocates the safeguarding peoples' right to live a fearless, hunger free and respectable life. This economic justice vision believes to ensure livelihood for all as well as develop mutual trust and respect. It believes in the transformation from evil and selfish to the gentle and generous human persons.

Although economic justice vision recognizes the profit earning, it also advocates effective control over accumulation of wealth beyond a ceiling – a line of wealth. In this regards it antagonize dishonesty, fraud and crime or similar others acts used for accumulation of wealth. The economic justice vision is for living a true, simple, transparent and decent life. If economic justice vision is implemented, it will also make society free from liquor trade provided that society collectively and consensually decides that. The society will also be made free from narcotics, superstitions, gambling, prostitution, begging and other similar sources of earning. The rationality behind all these is to ensure the criterion of economic justice, which is not found in other doctrines. Specific need of justice is for the disputes. Economic needs are the foundations of all disputes. Economic justice is a basic need right from birth to the death. Economic resources are required for everything to live in a human society simply for *Roti, Kapda aur Makan* (food, cloth and house). One can quit the luxuries, not the basic needs. Conflict between needs and luxuries is no doubt basic reason behind the strife. A comprehensive justice can cause interdependence and reconciliation in the society.

The vision of economic justice is not against the interests of any class, person or the society. While it advocates fear-free and respectful life to the vulnerable, it also professes life of prosperity, safety and prestige for all. It envisions a real citizenry by liberating them from untruth, hypocrisy, stress and guilt. When ones wealth is translated into true bliss, it becomes a new life. Despite exploited, let they become capable, and the towering personalities emerge from their families. Instead of treating as conspiratorial and exploitative, society start treating them as the talented member and guardian. Faith and mutual respect as well as peace will strengthen. It is the juncture where citizens follow the system voluntarily without imposition, enforcement and fear. Prosperity will increase and everyone will receive from its right of ownership to the natural resources.

Hence, the Economic Justice vision is far better than rest of existing ideologies. It also is an ideal system that is possible. It can also be the basis of a prosperous world order.

CHAPTER 14

ENVIRONMENT AND ITS IMPACT ON ECONOMY

Besides assessing the impact of economic justice on the society, it is also imperative to evaluate its effect on the environment. Without a favorable and flourishing environment, a happy life cannot be imagined. Therefore importance of the environment cannot be ignored for a happy society.

Environment not only provide us the abundance of all the natural resources for our consumption, many environmental phenomena such as seasons, water, air, sunlight etc. also remain friendly for the welfare of human beings. Current situation related to environment is very bad and worrisome. The ozone layer which is called the earth's protective shell has developed many holes in it. It is happening because industries producing toxic and harmful gases in large quantities. Likewise, many liquid or solids coming out of large factories are polluting the earth's water, soil and air and making them poisonous. Due to heavy burning of drugs, pesticides, chemical fertilizers and mineral oils, environmental conditions have become more alarming. Many social scientists, environmental experts, scientists and ideologues continue to alert the society about the horrific consequences of environmental degradation. But their warning does not have any effect on the people who are doing so; rather they keep violating the existing laws.

It is not that people who commit such crimes do not know the impact. But it has become a compulsion for them too. The fierce competition in the market has forced them to manufacture and produce high quality materials and sell them at cheaper prices. If they don't, they cannot survive in the market. Hence, they not only violate social duty and ethics, but also violate the penal laws. They know if caught, they might have to undergo jail sentence, punishment and financial loss. The problem cannot be solved by only blaming them for such a situation, because the main fault lies in the system, not with the individuals.

The solution to the problem lies in the mechanism based on 'economic justice'. The main reason for the deterioration of the environment is uncontrollable, unnecessary, harmful, dangerous, excessive production, and no restriction of society on the producers. Therefore, instead of producing item needed for welfare for society, producers produce such things which give them maximum profits.

The greed of earning maximum profit is the most important element that motivates them to do all kinds of wrong practices. Every person is in search for a shorter way to become rich quickly. This unbridled tendency among people is the root of all crimes, disputes and problems. There is hardly any religious book, saint, Mahatma, sociologist or humanist philosopher who has not prohibited people from the greed of immense profiteering.

The concept of auspicious benefit (Shubh Labh) in Indian tradition can be considered as the best example. In Indian culture, people on both side of their door write Shubh Labh. Businessmen, traders, farmers too write Shubh Labh on their safes, account book, equipment, and their source of livelihood. Today we, the Indians, are following our tradition, but do not understand its philosophical message. It has a clear meaning that the benefit is of two types: one 'auspicious' (Shub) and the other is 'inauspicious' (Ashubh). An auspicious profit is that which enrich the society and also the person. It is obtained not by violating the other person's rights, stealing or taking wrong advantage of compulsion of a person or causing damage to the environment and the nature or committing conspiracy, but gained by doing justice to all others. The profit obtained by the opposite methods is an 'inauspicious' profit. The meaning of writing Shubh Labh on homes and livelihood means that the home owner declares before the society that whatever wealth lies in his house is pure and auspicious. The feeling of not concealing anything from society is clearly implicit in it.

The longing for property to any extent is the root cause of the destructive trend, prevention of which is essential for social order. On the basis of justice, if a line is drawn to limit the accumulation of wealth, it will be an added advantage. The concept of economic justice improves the deficit of the current economy. According to this ideology, every citizen has the fundamental right to own the wealth up to a ceiling, and if one possesses wealth more than the ceiling, one is debtor to the society for that excessive wealth like a tenant or shareholder in a society. Therefore, on the wealth beyond line of wealth, one will have to pay tax or royalty at a decided rate of interest through a fair and transparent mechanism. He or she will have to pay the particular wealth tax/royalty until possesses the wealth beyond line of wealth. This implemented systematically will also curb tendency of greed in a person. Thereafter, one will do the work or business by keeping in mind the reality, justice and social welfare instead of accumulating extraordinary wealth. He or she will follow the impact on the environment and the laws related to it. Instead of aiming to get maximum income, he or she will produce consumables by ensuring social wellbeing. He or she will do complete justice to the employees and workers, and will not take advantage of their compulsions or weaknesses. In the name of market competition, he or she will not manufacture or produce substandard or bogus products rather one will produce materials of good quality and will sell these it to society at the justified price.

In such a situation, a complete different environment will be built up in the society. A lifestyle of harmless production will be developed which will enrich the environment. The cultural acts for example 'Havan' and 'Yajna' in Hindu societies that make the environment pure and prosperous, will earn a new space in the society. Their justification will also be understood by all. The awareness about duty towards society which has been completely ignored today will be awakened in the mind of every citizen. Thus the concept of economic justice will have a favorable impact on the environment.

As far as the impact on the entire economy of the country is concerned, that too will be very positive. The economy of any country depends on the balance of all its organs. These organs are production, exchange, distribution and consumption. Their imbalance creates a variety of ills, problems and crimes in the society. The ultimate utility or significance of any kind of production is selling to consumers.

Any production which cannot be consumed has no value. If production is less than demand, it leads to black marketing and profiteering in the society. And the excesses production creates destructive conditions for economic recession and environment. The less production is painful for consumers whereas excess production ruins producers. Due to excess production, growers suffer huge loss and many industries are shut down. Due to this, many workers, laborers and raw material as well as other required inputs sellers for agricultural producers and traders will also lose their livelihood and employment. The current system is not true to both these situations. The industries and trade whose production is in shortage in the market take unfair advantage by plundering the consumers; while the industries whose production is more than the demand in the market are distressed due to lack of demand for their products. There are also big producers who adopt anti-social methods and means by setting their products into fire, throwing them into the sea or destroy them to prevent price decline of the product in the market. This situation, however, can completely be changed in the system based on economic justice vision. In this system extreme desire to accumulate wealth will be curtailed through implementing one-tax system on the wealth above the line of wealth. Besides, the share of the national income in the form of a dividend will be paid to all the citizens regularly. Due to this, there will be no shortage in the income of citizens. Their pockets will remain full. It will make a huge increase in their workforce. This will also increase the demand for consumable items in the market, thus increasing the work of all the producers and traders too. Every item created by them will be sold at the demanded prices. Due to heavy demand, the market will move out of the cities and reach to the villages and the people living there will get the income along with other benefits. By increasing purchasing power, the effects of recession will end. All people will get prosperous. People would like to produce and trade items of good quality. Due to freedom from various types of tax, there will be big and unimaginable changes in the nature of the economy. Furthermore, government(s) will get benefit due to saving time and labor usually consumed in maintaining accounts of various kinds of taxes. The amount saved due to this, will be utilized to maintain cheap prices of consumer goods for common people. Consumers will get rid of the problem of inflation. Thus, the economy of the country will be flawless, clean, transparent, straightforward, truthful and free from corruption. All the dimensions of prosperity will be left behind in the new system as it will provide the full benefit of growth to every citizen.

CHAPTER 15

TAXATION IN INDIA, ETHICS AND SOCIAL TRANSFORMATION

The current taxation in India is poor, complex as well as contradictory, incomplete and unjust therefore it would not be wrong to call it a curse on the society. It is root cause of fallacies, hypocrisy, fraud and conspiracies. Despite being costly in terms of operational cost or system expenditure, the taxation system does not generate optimum revenues. A deficit budget every year is an open example. The legal, procedural and structural drawbacks of existing taxation system cause black-money, corruption and inflation. This also has added further expenditure of the persons through largely growing charter accountancy. In fact the existing taxation-system itself creates many problems for society, however it fallaciously claims for solving the issues and problems. This has caused mental, physical, moral, economic and spiritual losses to the society. Instead of directing the citizens to the honesty, it forces them to choose path of dishonesty.

It is worthwhile to analyze criterion of justice, ethics and humanity in the taxation process. The citizens today are taxed on each and every item of their use. Even essentials goods and services are being taxed. The poorest are not excluded from such taxation. On one hand, the government announces numerous exemptions for the poorer, while on the other hand it takes back the exemptions by taxing the essential goods and services. A hungry person, a beggar, even a dead body have not been exempted from the tax. This adds insult to the injuries of the people who already are living a miserable life. The poorest populate over 50 percent in the country. They are unable to get two times food despite working hard.

The dark aspect of this is while the poorest is being taxed, the richest is bestowed with different kinds of generosity in many contexts. It includes tax exemption on the taxable good and services as well as the loopholes that lower the value of taxable assets. Besides, the law of the country supports the rich to keep confidentiality of their assets details.

In the light of economic justice vision, the rich should be taxed more because wealth is identity of the rich, not the income. While this taxation system instead taxing all forms of wealth amicably, it taxes alone the income to higher extent. Therefore, a middle class is over taxed in the country meanwhile rich is under-taxed. Middle class does not only meet the living through their income, it also saves the income for special as well as futuristic requirements that include children's upbringing and their education, emergencies, marriages, funerals and other social as well as human obligations. Therefore, the existing taxation system despite elevating the middle class, it makes them poor and put them under debt. The upper middle class faces the issues of extra expenditure. This is not matter of consideration for taxation system. It even does not hesitate to tax poor, the loaned ones and those who are undergoing the crises or emergencies. This is the unethical and inhumane practice.

A person should have full control on its income, expenditure and consumption. Income should only be taxed when a person saves more than needs, special and futuristic requirements as well as emergencies; however the existing taxation system is not concerned with that. Another dark aspect is it forces persons to sell their properties for unpaid income taxes. The present system even forces the troubled people to sell their property to recover income tax. On the contrary, it provides procedural mechanism to the rich for tax evasion through filing income tax returns. Public has no idea how disastrous it is for the society. This impacts adversely on the society whether income tax returns are filed honestly or fallaciously. Because of the procedural flaws and mechanism, even the President, Prime Minister, Speaker of Lok Sabha (House of Common) or the Chief Justice of the Supreme Court has to file income tax return having inaccurate data. Therefore, the custodians of the country are also pushed by flawed procedures and mechanisms to process inaccurate detail. Thus, industrialists, businesspersons, bureaucracy, parliamentarians and landlords deceive the society through filing income details. Although the root cause in filling the fallacious details during income tax returns is the flawed laws, procedures and mechanisms, but these are enforced to the fullest. In fact, the law-makers are the real culprits. The system is full of flaws.

Unfortunately, despite all the flaws, the existing taxation system does not collect the revenues that governments require. A large amount of revenues from income tax is spent on its collections system. This further lowers the quantum of net revue. A small amount is left for the government expenditures. According to the official details, government has to spend two-thirds of annual budget on the non-development expenditure; therefore it does not have enough revenues to spend on development. For the rest unavoidable expenditures, governments either borrow or prints more currency, which causes highly adverse impacts on the economy.

In the light of economic justice vision, the tax has to be levied on the wealth that exceeds the average line of wealth, which ultimately is to tax handful millionaire. If this one-tax system is applied, majority of the citizens will get rid of all the taxes. Apart from this, the revenues will be more than that of existing ones, therefore besides meeting the government expenditure; each citizen will also be able to receive INR 10000 per month from the annual revenue savings which can be said the lifelong monthly dividend for every citizen. This taxation regime will be true to all parameters of justice based taxation.

It is the economy related legal framework flaws and the concept associated with them, supplemented by the law of wealth confidentiality of citizens that cause economic disaster in the revenues collection perspective. Private wealth owners evade taxes by manipulating the valuation of their assets. The patriots should think on this. Without introducing change in these laws, no significant improvement in the economy is possible. Theoretically, a nation is a vast family, and the citizens are its members. A person can be competent; however as a member of the family that is called nation, one should have fundamental and birthright to respect and dignity devoid of competence and similar specialties. It is the responsibility of family head, called leader of the nation as well as of wise and literate to make it happen. Without this the real nation building cannot be made.

CHAPTER 16

ORIGIN AND OWNERSHIP OF INTEREST

'Interest' as well as its origin and hold have a tremendous impact on the economy. If an economy is compared with a running horse, the interest is its rein holder. A horse runs in certain direction, and the person holding its reins determines it direction. Generally everyone is familiar with what simply the interest use to be. Interest is the amount, which borrower offers or pays back additionally along with the borrowed amount to the lender. One can simply call it rent paid on the borrowed money to the lender similar to tenant that pays out to the house owner. Similarly, the debtor pays interest to the lender on the basis of a fixed rate and fixed time.

All economists believe that interest is not a production because lender does not undertake activity to produce through lending. Lender to them is the owner of interest, along with loaned amount, only because a lender saves money by sacrificing his consumption needs or profit making activities. Saving money requires to sacrifice one's consumption or production oriented as well as other sorts of investments. If someone does not save money, he or she will not be able to accumulate wealth, which is a capital. This argument is fallacy. In fact, origin of the interest lies in the role of money in production, exchange and consumption. It is a known fact that money or capital plays very important role in all kinds of productions such as agriculture, industry, and livestock. Capital is also needed for exchange, trade and transactions. Similarly, many times a person needs accumulated wealth for unforeseen emergency. Therefore, today it is almost impossible to produce anything without money in association with fulfilling basic needs for consumption. If a person does not have his or her own accumulated wealth, he or she has no option excepting borrowing from others. And, why one will be lending without any income? Without income none will lend or tender the monetary assistance.

There is no security of loan payback within agreed timeframe. Usually loaned amount is risk prone. Therefore, the only secure option for lender is the interest on the loan. This is the reason lender determines the rate of interest on the basis of the sacrifice of his or her need, compulsions, other investment options along with the risk factor. Therefore, in economic terms, the interest can be said a kind of opportunity cost which lender takes from the borrower. Hence, the amount which the lender collects in the form of interest is a benefit or profit for the lender. Clearly, this benefit is not lieu of labor. It is earned from a needy and money scarce borrower. Besides, lender also decides the timeframe of loan return.

Simply an interest on a loan can be said a reward or benefit to the lender for sacrificing needs as well as other profit-making investments.

In reality, it is not appropriate to call interest a reward of sacrifice. A person can accumulate wealth only if conditions are favorable. A person accumulates wealth due to the uncertainty of the future and the fear of uncertainty about his or her capabilities. Every person needs constant consumption to remain alive and he fulfills this need through his or her constant income. In favorable conditions, if the person's income is more than the requirement of his consumption, he can store wealth for future. In adverse conditions, when his income is less than the requirements, he cannot save the money despite his desire to do so. So it is wrong to associate the accumulation of wealth with renunciation.

The key aspect in the origin of interest is the role of capital in industry, business or trade. In a bid to earn money, a person has to approach a resourceful person, firm or organization, to establish his own business. If someone, today, does not have required money usually there is no other option than that of borrowing money on interest. If the loan is taken for business purpose, the borrower adds the interest payments in the expenditure on the production, which increases production cost, thereby increase the price of commodities and services. Finally, the consumer pays for the interest on the business.

The entire economy is focused on the transaction. Everyone person tries to earn more of which the transactions are the key financial activity. Besides competence, risk-taking, capital and other resources of an individual, economic environment also play an important role.

When a person receives more income and spends less, it means that he or she is taking more from the society but returning less to it which leads to the accumulating wealth. One purchases goods or services in little quantity and sells more goods or services of one's owns. The adverse consequences of purchasing little quantity of others' good or services are faced by the producers of those goods, thus cause decline in the demand for these goods and services resulting into reduction in the profit. Large manufacturers also do the same. They produce at large scale that reduces the production cost, lowers prices and returns larger volume of profit in comparison with the small manufacturers. With this, while their prosperity increases, the other people in the society have to suffer the loss.

The accumulation of wealth at higher scale cost the interest of others. We get all the means of consumption and production from natural resources. Natural resources are in limited quantity in the world, therefore when a person accumulates the wealth at higher scale, the rest suffer. A person who accumulates more wealth is responsible for others' loss. Since all people have an equal right on the natural resources, therefore every person has right to acquire natural resources for his or her consumption, not for accumulation of property and assets more than consumable need.

In the contemporary era of scientific advancements, the role of capital and capital based resources has increased. The inventions and introduction of modern technology in the process of production and services, means of commodity production and business strategies along with mechanisms have changed. The new technology has undertaken role of millions of human laborers. Hence, a new technical laborer, smallest in quantity, can produce tremendously large volume of production. This has caused price reduction however to no avail of consumers. The producers decide the sale price based on the gross expenditure on per unit of the production, which also include loan interests and rentals utilized by the producers for the production. Eventually, the beneficiaries are capital holders and losers are the consumers, poor and unemployed laborers who due to contemporary era of technological advancements have become unemployed. Contrary to this, the technological advancements are proportionate with the increase in the role of capital due to large quantity productions, low prices and increase in the profit - a would-be capital itself. Also, high scale decrease in the demand of non-technical labor has caused unemployment and low wages.

The bases of profit are the free exchange and sell of production. If exchange and production are not free then the additional benefits from resources or money cannot be obtained. Therefore, each consumer who is playing his role in free production and exchange through consumption of the products should be equally entitled for the additional benefits he cause for the producers who is capital holders and key beneficiary. If they do not get the benefit, the consumption will not increase; therefore demand will remain constant or probably may decrease. In the conclusion, that interest is result of collective and integrated economic process, it is not only due to sacrificing needs or the possible investment opportunities. Therefore, benefits generated out of interest collected on loaned amount should have stakeholder beneficiaries- a collective. The lenders without any doubt should receive the loaned amount which is called principal amount; however the interest over it is also a shareholding of collective, stakeholders.

Finally, the income from the interest should be considered a collective income of the society, which is the only justice-based-reality regarding the interest on the loans. Hence, there should also be an arrangement to pay the collective, the society their part in the income. This will advantage in ending economic disparity. It will also help ending the both extremes – the extreme richness and poverty. The income of the person will fundamentally be based on the labor, in any form, he or she has provides.

CHAPTER 17

PRIVATE WEALTH RIGHTS

Whether a person should have the right to own private wealth? It is a serious question for society.

There are serious differences in the society over this question and the world is divided over it. We have to examine this question from justice, sociological, economic and psychological perspectives. Let us begin with the sociological viewpoint. We need to examine whether the right to wealth is a fundamental right of a person or it is conferred by a system. The purpose of social order is to provide maximum freedom to everyone as much as possible. Since right of freedom is broader, therefore a minute violation of it intrudes the freedom of the other. Therefore, society sees such a violation inappropriate, and worth punishable. Think on it. You will see concept of equality beneath this fundamental right of freedom. Besides, it is also observed that equality is not permanent. In the context of substances offered by the nature, equality means everyone's equal rights on all natural-substances. Therefore, the axioms of this right depend on the availability of natural resources in proportionate equation with the populace. Besides, the breadth of the right varies according to the situations. Example, if water is in abundance, none will be asked for the quantity of water use. In water scarcity, however, quantity of the water use will be determined and persons will be asked to abide by the rule or norm. One of the fundamentals for this regulation would be the provision of water according to the current necessities alone. Ignoring requirements of the present, nobody can be allowed to accumulate wealth for the future needs. Therefore, the accumulation or storage of natural resource for the future should only be allowed when the present needs of all are met. This should also be applied to the right to private wealth.

Wealth accumulation fundamentally is rooted in the storage of natural resources for future consumption, which one does after the fulfillment of present needs. This further reduces the resources. Meanwhile, the remaining persons engage or sell more labor to earn livelihood. They have to face troubles caused by resource scarcity. Storage of produce leaves adverse impacts on the nature for the further production of the resources. If the resources are not stored on the pretext of future, nature can be saved from unnecessary exploitation. It will maintain the richness of nature and availability of resources. Therefore, despite storing resources in the name of future needs, these should only be utilized to fulfill the present. This is one side of the picture. On the other side, we have to dig deep into why does people save? The reasons are psychological and practical.

Human desire is to earn maximum consumables with minimum labor. This has developed human civilizations. Uncertainty for the future is another factor for the resource saving. The natural resources for human consumption are limited, and their volume has changed along with the time and according to spatiality. Practiced in abundance, persons accumulate at larger scale, and consume from the accumulation during scarcity. Besides, a person's capacity to work also changes in the disease or due to accidents in which he or she is unable to work, and has to suffer in the absence of resource storage. Similarly, one's ability to work changes as one becomes older. In youth one is highly capable, while in childhood and old age the work capacity is low. Therefore, one-time accumulation helps persons during the adversaries. Since situations happen and wither away in certain period, the human tendency to accumulate property must also be recognized. Prohibiting wealth accumulation will also be unfair because doing so will violate fundamental right of freedom to independently consume his or her earned resources. It will derail the entire social system. A path for collective benefits and income to all is required. A system should resist the adverse impacts of accumulation of private wealth, and also ensure the right to save or accumulate for the future needs. In a bid to reach this milestone, an appropriate ceiling on the holding private wealth be imposed. There should be ceiling based on the average wealth owning in a society which should be called line of wealth.

Now, see the things in today. Can today's economy be called an interdependent or collective economy?

All economic activities are interdependent. One person's actions for economic pursuits depend on others, and this process decrease the production cost. Besides, accumulation of wealth has also increased. Technological advancement has increased capacity to work and produce; therefore more production is achieved with small amount of labor. A person's income in a interdependent economy depends on his resources, not the labor. Therefore, the big resourceful earn more directly proportionate with the volume of resources. Meanwhile, *resourceless* person earn adversaries. Large scale production due to modern technology has reduced opportunities for *resourcesless* laborer to engage in the process of production, thereby earning. *Incomeless* face miseries and socio-economic inequality widens. Hence, in a interdependent economy accumulated wealth adds up in the inequality everyday. Therefore, a conflict between ideologies of right to private wealth and persons' equal rights has emerged. Private wealth has violated the universality of equal rights. This, the most important matter of our times, should be addressed justly. In the line of justice, human labor should be determining factor for income generation, not the use of technologies. Ultimately, we need to distribute the income generated from the resources in a manner to maintain equality in the society and the system.

The nature of the current economy is determined by the following factors:

- Freedom of creation, production and exchange
- Monetary system
- Personal ownership approach

- Energy-produce from natural resources
- Modern technology used for production, transport, traffic, telecommunication etc.

Because of these factors, manufacturing of goods in huge quantity, transportation, information, direct exchange of goods and services have become very simple and comprehensive aspects of today's economy. The use of modern technology in the economy has reduced human role in the economy related processes. However, it is clear that it has enhanced the wages and other benefits for a small number of human involved in the process of economy. Significant savings by relatively larger number of human is impossible without this; however the income of this should also be provided to society on equal basis.

How the profit from the resources is calculated? A question according to the economic realities indeed. Current economic system is the only answer. When income is earned with help of modern technology, persons attempt to accumulate resources because of their increase income. An increase in income is enhanced purchase power therefore demands of various productions increase along with the demand of money itself. This increase in demand of money is manifested into the interest on the money. Interest paid according to prevailing interest rate is an additional income (without laboring) in the interdependent economy. Therefore, the income received from interest on loan or rentals is in its origin an income or saving earned from labor. Hence this profit should a collective income of society.

At the moment, the interest on the lending is solely owned by the lender who is fundamentally wealthy.

Whatsoever forms of interest do exist in a society is not equally distributed to all -- the consumers and the poor -- rather it is based on being proportionate to the volume of wealth, which also is a form of economic injustice.

To ensure an equal distribution among the society of the income earned through interest, a tax should be imposed on the bases of prevailing interest rate on the wealth, the revenue out of which should equally be distributed to all in a society.

In this system, all kinds of adverse effects and impacts are result of excessive accumulation of wealth. By introducing this new tax, the private wealth right related issues will be settled forever. This will play an important role in liberating the society, and a new social bond will grow based on justice and natural equality.

CHAPTER 18

IMPACT OF ECONOMIC JUSTICE ON DEMOCRACY

Democracy is a system of governance in which adult citizens form system of state through their elected representatives. In democracy all citizens become voters of the country once they reach the age for adult franchise. This right does not require any examination or qualification. A vote of all citizens is equal. It is a basic political right of every citizen using which one can choose his favorite representatives.

In election the candidate who gets more votes than the other competing candidates becomes an elected representative. The elected representatives choose their president, prime minister, speaker of the house(s) through popularly elected representatives of the legislative houses called Lok Sabha (house of commons, lower house) in India. Meanwhile, senators for the Rajya Sabha (Senate), as well as judges of the higher judiciary are chosen by the elected government.

Voters have the right to choose the country's lawmakers and legislators that are called Member Parliament (MP) for central government in India, while Member Legislative Assembly (MLA) for states (provinces). They are elected to make laws and every kind of reform in the system of a country. They can also amend the existing laws. They can make a new constitution. The formation of federal, central, and state or provincial governments is also done by the citizens through vote. The elected representatives form government, which called the executive that executes the business of country though a cabinet, led by a Prime Minister in center and the Chief Minister in India. The elected representatives also select the judges however constitution and procedures are already devised in a bid to avoid conflict between both – the executive and judiciary. The final authority to make policies and rules for governance lies with the parliament (centre) and legislative assemblies (state). Meanwhile these laws and policies have to be implemented and executed by the executive called government. The executive is fully accountable to the legislature; therefore it has to take approval of the legislature for executive policies, budget and key decisions.

Basically adult citizen transfer their right to rule themselves in a country through electing the legislature that forms the government. Therefore, it is believed that democracy is a form of government is run by the people and for the public. It is a voter's prorogate to choose one out of many candidates for the parliament through elections. The election for representatives is chosen for a time period. The voters vote every time when the elected representatives term period ends and the elections are held for the electing new representatives. Therefore, after completing their term period, elected representatives have to go back to the voters. Whose work is satisfactory in the view of the voters get re-elected, and with whom voters are unsatisfied, are rejected and stand unelected. This way, voters control the elected representatives.

Although in many countries citizens have adult franchise, but there is a huge difference between the rules and administrative structure of governance amongst them. Despite all the variations, it is considered a democratic system, because of universality of adult franchise. Once adult, a person's becomes part of political process. A person naturally acquires vote right once he becomes adult. The adult franchise is a real identity of democracy because all citizens acquire right to vote once they turn eighteen.

Therefore, the foundation of democracy is equality among the people. Equality is also the foundation of justice. On the basis of justice for all, the democratic system is considered the best in the world. However for an ideal democracy political right is not the only agency for democratic practices. People should also have fundamental economic rights through the system as all the people have equal right on the resources of a country. This is the real asset or wealth of a nation that forms the entire economic system of a country where citizens should get all the resources for utilization through optimum labor. There should be no discrimination or injustice to anyone in a system that claims democracy.

Fundamental economic rights should also be conferred to every citizen of the country at the time of birth. Without this, one's life cannot be protected. When a person is unable to have requirements for survival, his political rights becomes meaningless.

Present democratic system therefore is incomplete. It will become complete only when every citizen in a country shall have the equal basic economic rights, which naturally become conferred once a baby born. An equal economic right should begin immediately after birth unto the death. It should not be conditioned with qualifications, abilities, efficiency, happiness, or any similar criterion. Resultantly, no poor or vulnerable face hindrances in the needs as well as wishes. Citizens with more qualifications and/or competitiveness should also have freedom to increase their economic prosperity but without intruding into or undermining the fundamental economic rights of others. The nonexistence of equal economic rights in a political system, and conferring equal political right to vote is the major drawback of democratic system, which needs to be addressed. In a deep analysis, the key reason behind conflicts is directly related to compulsory human consumption. Once consumption need of everyone is fulfilled, a political right like vote will be exercised truly. A person whose economic needs are not fulfilled, his or her political rights are futile. A complete democracy, which may be called an ideal democratic system, cannot be developed mere on the basis of political rights.

An economic system based on economic justice perfectly suits the very much concept of democracy. It will eliminate the flaws in the contemporary democratic system. After getting freedom of fundamental economic right for livelihood, a citizen will perform his democratic role appropriately and heartily. It will space out a healthy real democracy. Resultantly, the concept of a democratic system will be drawback free as well as complete.

Power of money, today, dominates the contemporary political scene everywhere, which has curtailed and intruded into the freedom of speech for the persons. Through power of the accumulated money or monetary assets, people's thoughts, honesty, loyalty, patriotism and obligations have become commodities in the social and political markets. The modus operands to get something on the basis of greed, even killing opponents in a bid to wield more has become phenomenal in the crime scenes within the democracies. An atmosphere of fallacies, untruth, lies, mistrust and hypocrisy is created in such a way that fair and responsible citizens get confused and de-tracked. In such an atmosphere, one cannot think of an ordinary person's stance and stand for truth, justice and rights for a long period.

The deteriorations in the contemporary democratic system are due to high volume monitory and financial use in the personal, economic and political life. False and baseless propaganda overpowers the truth and influences the decision of voters. Parliamentarians or legislators elect through the vote however bagging more votes they use money excessively, therefore voters' decision is influenced, and hence they become slave or *freedomless* voters. In this context, the parliamentarians or legislators are not the real and true representative of the public. India also today is undergoing this dilemma of democracy. Despite being the world's largest democracy, the naked dance of using money to mint votes has become identity of the democratic system. Literally, criminals and mafias have established their influence in the legislature in India. A grand decline in trust and respect for the legislature and the executive in the public has become a bitter truth of our times. The elected law-makers are not performing their responsibilities towards the people and the country. They legislate non-right, unjust, interest-groups favoring and discriminatory laws. Commoner is being victimized and looted.

In the light of unbearable realities of contemporary democracy including and especially of India, the fundamental equal economic rights are niche to translate the election based political system into a democracy. A complete democracy with fundamental economic rights along with the political rights would really be the actual justice.

CHAPTER 19

IMPACTS ON STATE & MINIMAL GOVERNMENT

It is duty of the state to ensure full protection of all the citizens in the country. It should also protect the right of every person. The state has the responsibility to ensure the proper utilization of all the natural resources of the country and to prevent it from misuse. For this, it is the responsibility of the state to make suitable economic policies for achieving an ideal system, as well as to implement them properly. For this, it is necessary that all the means of production should be fully utilized so that required maximum production is achieved. It is also the responsibility of the government to ensure fair distribution of the production among everyone in the society.

The government has huge responsibility of building the entire economy system along with internal and external security of the country. For its implementation, the people in power needed a large number of additional bureaucrats. In such a situation, while power has become highly centralized in hands of authorities, commoner has become powerless. The interference of governments in the lives of the people has greatly increased. People sitting in the governance and bureaucracy misuse their administrative powers and rob commoners. Besides, they deliberately interfere in the work of those who perform their duty rightfully. They also protect and promote criminals and those who does wrong. All citizens, who do not believe in their lies, have to bear the brunt of their conspiracies and wrath.

In order to fulfil their huge responsibilities, governments also require voluminous administrative staff that does not only requires huge amount of revenues but it is also difficult to keep them under control. The larger the administrative structure, lesser the administrative efficiency. In the big and complex administrative process and laws, common citizens experience extreme problems and get engulfed in it. Different laws, their misuse and the centralization of power make commoners like slaves of State. They remain unaware of many misdeeds of governance. Even after having knowledge, they become only a silent spectator in absence of legal right. The concept of economic justice, however, will solve all these problems properly, because the big excuse or reason for the governments is the economy related obligations. It has made many departments to collect the taxes. Additionally, various departments are formed to meet and protect the economic interests of different sections of the society. Likewise, for the weaker sections of the society, such as workers, peasants, Dalits (untouchables in South Asia), Tribals, Non-Tribals, backward castes, minorities and the majority many different laws and departments have been created. In addition to poverty, unemployment, inflation, education, health and justice, there is large number of laws and departments for maintaining law and order in the society.

Economic justice vision, envisions one-tax – the wealth tax on the excessive wealth beyond the ceiling in the Line of Wealth – that is detailed here as one-tax system. There is also a system of dividend to be transferred to all the citizens. It will make government completely free from the huge burden of financial liabilities. Most of the people's key problems are economic and these all are the resulted by scarcity of money among the poor majority. Dividend is the best solution for it. After getting the dividend, most of the conflicts occurring amongst the people will also come to an end. It will also help the government to permanently shut down many departments established to address these problems. If this kind of situation is created, the government's work will be reduced so that it will be able to pay full attention towards the internal and external security of the country. With the small administrative structure, its efficiency will increase, while corruption will reduce. In general, the governance and administrative responsibilities as well as liabilities will greatly decrease, and need for various laws will end. This will establish good governance. People will be more independent and happy. This will highly impact the political structure of the country. The continuous fair distribution of wealth in the society will reduce the accumulation of wealth. Although economic inequality will exist however within the radius of justice. All the people in the society will have such prosperity that they can make their lives free from incapability and will develop their talents. With the end of many conflicts in society, people will apply their energy to strengthen education, knowledge and health. This will create better, sensible, just and peaceful citizens.

This will make every citizen an alert and sensible voter, who will understand his or her responsibilities well. It would be very difficult to fool him with covetousness, fear, superstition or pressure. Such conscious voters will seriously deliberate on all kinds of problems and on their basic solutions. They will decide what laws should be made in the country and what should be changed or eliminated for betterment of the public.

The good impact will be that qualified people, scholar, patriots and thinkers will be able to reach legislature. Their goal will not be to enjoy the pleasure of the power or to fulfill any selfishness, but to take society towards betterment. The people of the country will have a real representation in the legislature, who will have full control over the executive. The government will also honor public sentiments and will act accordingly. The bureaucracy will also work honestly so that people will get rid of problems like corruption, negligence, injustice and delays.

Since internal problems will be solved in country, the government will give full attention towards world politics; strengthening armed forces for the security; and will make arrangements of weapons required for it. There will be no scarcity of funds for these matters.

CHAPTER 20

QUESTIONS & ANSWERS ON ECONOMIC JUSTICE SYSTEM

Many questions can come in one's mind on the system based on the economic justice vision, it is necessary therefore to answer some possible important questions. Determination of Line of Wealth instead of Line of Poverty; the concept of imposing one-tax system in a country only on those possessing more than median Line of wealth; and distribution of revenues through one-tax system among all people in form of dividends are entirely new concepts.

Questions mentioned here are out of many asked by the scholars, activists and commoners in India.

Q. Does distribution of dividend among all the citizens by imposing taxes on a few is not like giving persons money without any efforts. Is it not a form of freebies?

A. Not freebies; it is a justice with all citizens. Citizens of the country are equally owners of the country's resources. The natural resources of a country are the real wealth or economic valuables. Citizens have equal right on the income coming out of these.

Q. But, people have to work for earning income in any way?

A. Income for a person has two factors – resources and labor. On the basis of justice, the income from the natural resources should be shared among all the citizens, besides they will also receive wages of labor they do.

Q: Will this not make people lazy?

A: Implementation of one-tax system based on economic justice will not have the same impact on all. A small number of persons may become slow, not lazy, in the production or services process, meanwhile rest majority will engage with more interest in the productive processes and the labor. On the contrary, a vast majority today due to unaffordability can neither develop required skills and capability nor become qualified for appropriate labor in the technology driven contemporary economy. Hunger kills talent in the childhood. Isn't it an unaffordable loss society? For instance, if some people will become lazy, at least they will not become Naxalites[2], terrorists, heinous criminals, separatists and pessimists. They will also have the hope of living and their enthusiasm for social order will increase. If society remains free from the destructiveness, will it not be more beneficial than meager loss loss due to a few lazy?

Q: Why not they should be given job instead of dividends?

A: Most people who talk about giving jobs to everyone today are ignorant. Industrial revolution kicked of advancement in science and technology therefore the entire structure of the economy has become mechanized and has unemployment human labor, which has also income and monetary meaning. Mechanized process and work is simple and easy however it has reduced human labor nine times than the traditional industrial economy. It has increased production tremendously but decreased employment drastically. Can 10 percent employers provide jobs to 90 percent jobless? If largest human labor is engaged, production surpasses demand for goods and services, therefore economies will slowdown causing grand recession as well as trade and commerce collapse.

---

2 A decades long armed conflict between government forces and Naxalism activists in India claiming Marxist ideology; however have failed to bring socialist revolution even in one district

Q. *Will they not become drug addicts or ruffian by getting freebies and illegitimate money?*

A. First and foremost, it is not illegal money; it is the right of ownership of natural resources that is completely justified. On a different note, government policies are responsible for an increase in addiction. On one hand, the governments through advertisements asks people to keep away from alcohol and intoxicants and launches the narcotics free campaign (*Nasha Mukti Abhiyan*), on the other hand it allow the same intoxicants to be sold legally. Irony that governments give lame excuses of revenue generation from the of narcotics sale. In the light of economic justice vision, elimination of all taxes, excepting newly defined wealth tax on wealth exceeding Line of Wealth is the way forward. It will also end scarcity of revenue for the governments. It would be easier for governments to have strict measures on all addictive substances. Punishments on narcotics sale should be legislated if society collectively and consensually decides so. This will not only reduce the tendency of narcotics consumption but will decrease this habit among the people. Similarly, extremism and criminality will decrease. Today many people are committing crime due to hunger, incline to narcotics along with crime because of injustice and dissatisfaction. The number of people who commit crimes due to the psychological tendency is in the limited scale.

Q. *The wealth is gained on the basis of talent and hard work. Is not it injustice to extract heavy taxes from them on the basis of Line of Wealth?*

LINE OF WEALTH

A. This is not an injustice. Neither earning on the basis of talent and hard work is wrong act, nor the due share of citizen in the wealth be taken by force. In the light of justice, a fixed rent or royalty will be taken from them on the excessive wealth. If all citizens have equal rights on all natural resources of the country, then every citizen will be justified to have property on the basis of average ceiling. Having more talent, intellect or physical energy does not mean to usurp natural resources rights of the weak persons, hence deprive them of their right to live. Injustice to the rich person will happen only when they are deprived of keeping wealth bellow the ceiling in accordance with Line of Wealth. Economic justice vision advocates taxing the wealth owned more than an average of wealth ownership in a society, which should be levied at the existing interest rate in a society, which is 8-10 percent annually. The remaining 90 to 92 percent of the wealth or its monetary equitant will remain with them. They will be independent and free to do according to their plans with the net wealth they do have after being taxed. The very same large wealthy persons pay various taxes. And, they don't have required degree of freedom and confidence as well as peace and security. They become victim of humiliation and blackmailing especially in developing and under-developed world. They along with their families feel insecurity. However, by implementing economic justice vision they will be fear-free of state-system, criminal mafias, miscreants etc. They will be able to do their business in more safe and peaceful environment. Just compare. Which system or situation will be better?

Q. Will not the economy of the country collapse if billions of rupees are distributed in the form of dividend?

A. The economy of the country will not collapsed rather it will become stronger, because every citizen will buy good of their consumption if they will get money as dividend. This will increase the demand for everything. This will bring revolution in the market. Industrialists, businessmen, farmers, cattle traders and many other services will fulfill this enormous demand. It will create a lot of work and everyone will be busy in it. Closed industry and business will also be revived. All their goods will be sold at the demanded prices. So there will be no need to cheat people. All people will be benefitted from their livelihood so that they will be happy. This sequence will go on continuously.

If we look deeply, we are talking about economy of a country with only taxing all forms of wealth more than ceiling for untaxed wealth holding called Line of Wealth. This will not reduce the prosperity of the country, but will increase it.

Q. What is the logic behind the increase in prosperity?

A: The prosperity of any country depends on the proper and maximum utilization of the means of production. Today, a large number of productive properties are lying unproductive in the country. It is because there is no loss on account of any hindrance or lack of special tax. The owner rather he get benefited by keeping it idle. Keeping useful property in the unproductive form leads to artificial reduction in the means of production, by doing so owners in fact increase its market prices and earn huge income. However, it is a huge loss to society. This reduces the production of the country and the country gets poorer. By imposing heavy one-tax on wealth, it will become a loss making to keep wealth non-productive. The owner will be able, in practice, to keep the wealth with him only when he earns more than the tax imposed on the wealth. With this, all the productive means of the country will be engaged in the production i-e business, trade, commerce and agricultural production. It will lead to the prosperity of the people as well as of the country.

Q. Will it not reduce the importance of labor?

A. The importance of labor will not decrease; rather its value will increase. Today the situation of labors is abysmal. They are victim of extreme poverty, deprivation and misery because they get highly low wages. The only reason for this is rivalry between labor and capital owner. People's income is related to their wealth, it is not a matter of hard work. The wealthy are living the life of luxury even by doing small amount work or labor; meanwhile the workers are forced to lead a life of scarcity and humiliation despite hard labor. By imposing one-tax system through which taxing wealth only, we will be reducing dominancy of wealth and wealthy, and distribute out of one-tax revenue as dividends to the citizens in a bid to strengthen weak, poor, and workers. By distributing dividends equally among citizens, the wages in the market will increase and interest rate on lending will decrease. Therefore, no laborer will work on low wages due to need and helplessness. Besides, he or she will also manage his or her matters with the employer. This will also enhance credibility and honor of labor and the laborers.

Q: Will not it increase the population of the country?

A: No, not at all. In fact it is the only humane and ideal way to check the increase in population. This is a serious psychological question, if we look at the situation around the world; the population crisis is only in poor countries. In developed countries, however, the situation is totally opposite. Inclination to have children is decreased enough in developed countries that the governments there have to appeal people to birth more children. The only reason behind this is mental that the poor wants more children and rich wants fewer. Because of power realities and aspects, the poor wants more children for his or her protection. Contrarily, the prosperous one does not feel insecure. In addition, poor is prone to ignorance and superstitions. Birth of a child, to them, is choice of God unlike prosperous one, who chose to have child according to their intention. A survey of population in India also confirms this.

In India, the birth rate is more among the illiterate and poor class of the society and in less among educated and prosperous sections. Therefore, if we want free the country from darkness of poverty, the population naturally will decrease; no coercive policy will be adopted.

Q. This will increase the demand of goods, which will cause the burden on nature, and ultimately on environment—already highly degraded. Will it not further worsen the situation?

A. It is a hypothetical thinking. One, the quantity of things of essential use like bread, cloth and house will increase; two, there will be a huge decline in the demand for high luxuries items most of them use to be pollution generators. The production of luxurious items is enormous. Natural resources are being used for the manufacturing and operation of luxury items. This is the biggest damage to our environment, along with the other anti-environment production. Rich use and purchase such goods and services more than their requirement. The enlivenment hazardous goods related to luxury are not naturally recycled; therefore continue polluting soil, water and air for the longer time. On the contrary, the food, cloth and house related goods are naturally recycled, hence after causing minute hazard to environment, undergoes the environmental revival. Commoners spend more money on their everyday needs, while rich spends more on luxuries. By implementing one-tax system, a broader wealth tax indeed, the expenditure on luxuries will reduce, which will also further immunize the population. In a situation we undergoing today, the society may ban the things that cause environmental hazards.

Q. Wealth will reduce the people' passion for work. Will this not weaken the economy?

A. Despite reduction in the passion for work, the greed and desire to accumulate more will reduce. And, this will be in the best interest of the society. Society does not control the production due market competition for the more profit. The production of goods does not solely depend on the need of the people; it fundamentally depends on the profiteering of the investor.

If anti-environmental production decline, society will be beneficiary; however means of production cannot be kept idle. Due to one-tax system, commoner will have more access to the natural resources and consumables, which will reduce the centralization of the means of production. Again, it will be in the interest of the society. Overall, the one-tax system will increase the country's total production, instead of falling.

Q: Due to broader wealth tax, will the rich and inverter not immigrate to other countries?

A: Thinking this way is meaningless. The investors prefer the places for their business that are secure, peaceful, and corporative governments and suitable governance. They prefer simple and transparent tax system and places where raw materials and large market are available. After one-tax system, the country itself will turn into such an investment friendly place. Although it is assumed, a few money minting businesspersons may immigrate elsewhere, they will have to sell their real assets at nominal prices. Moreover, where in world they will hide? Once economic justice vision is implemented, it will spread into the world. Because of investment friendly environment after economic justice implementation, the foreign investors will come to India. And the fugitives will have to face even complex, worse and humiliating situations abroad. If appropriate laws are made, the run-away of local businesspersons can be escaped as well. Even the laws for the ceiling on taking away money out of country can also be legislated.

Q. Why those who does not generate income despite having huge property, will pay the wealth tax?

A. It is not in the interest of both a wealthy persons and the society that the wealth remain unutilized. Should such property remain in their possession? It is in the interest of both that the wealth should be handed over to those who can utilize it properly. Therefore, by selling their assets, such persons will look for their areas of interests. A certain number of persons spent miserable life despite having property. It would be better if they sell the assets and happily lives with the money in their hands.

Q. Is not the limit on right to own property violates freedom of a person?

A. Freedom can never be unlimited. A person can be given freedom however for the sake of creating good system and enriching society. Equal freedom has to be based on justice, which ultimately means a median degree of freedom, simply an average equal freedom for all. In the economic justice vision, a secure freedom to have assets with flat-rate one-tax system is there. One-tax revenues are royalty to the society.

Q. *Will ending confidentiality of private property will not be interference in personal life?*

A. No. Because basically all natural resources is original economic sources and wealth, all other forms of resources, wealth, production and services are developed out of them. In this context, a person whom we call the owner of the wealth is only the one who labors on it. One takes raw materials from natural resources for the purpose of production, and thereby generates wealth in the form of income. Everyone has equal right on the natural resources. An increase in the private property will reduce the volume of the collective property in the society which ultimately will cause harm. Therefore, why not everyone should have right to know who is owning what and to what extent!

Q. *Government is already having details of everyone's property. Since governments are public representatives, will disclosure of information about one's assets be not unfair?*

A. The government is not the owner of the property in a country, it is only the representative of the society, or we can call it a type of manager of the property. The original owners are citizens. Will it not be wrong that while a manager has right to know about property, to investigate, to confiscate property, to arrest a person, but the owner does not have such rights? It is not a matter of arrogance and dishonesty. With this, the manager will become the master and the real owners (citizens) will become beggar. This is what happening today. The government today is openly misusing the law of privacy. It is facilitating with the rich, giving protection to the thieves and cheating society in partnership with them. It is conspiracy against the people of the country. The law of confidentiality of property is dangerous. There will be no harm to anyone by abolishing this law.

Q. *Will not it increase the work and expenditure of the government?*

A. You may be satisfied that government is already having the property details of citizens; however these details have to be given to the citizen. The persons, who seek other's wealth details, have to pay fees. The uninterested in others wealth details will not have such information. It is worthless to discuss. Examining income tax details, currently, huge monetary resources, time and labor are spend but the truth still remains unearthed. The generation of black money in the country is evident.

Q: *Will not thieves and robbers take advantage of the abolition of the law of confidentiality of property. Will not the owners of the property become vulnerable?*

A. If thieves capture power, what will then happen? What is going on today? Those in government create problem for law abiding citizens and contrarily protect the corrupt by hiding their misdeeds from the citizenry. Therefore, the corrupt escape public anger and the punishment by the law. If there is no confidentially, their misdeeds cannot be hidden from the society. This will give protection to law abiding citizens. Mischievous will have to face the fury. Truth will be common in the society; the practices of lying will end. Therefore, non-confidentiality of the wealth is in the interest of the society, not against it. Due to the confidentiality of the property, wealthy, ruler and bureaucrat conspire together to plunder the society. If the law of confidentiality is abolished, it will not be possible to hide the truth from the society. Even the secrecy about wealth does not remains unearth today of those who advocate the law of confidentiality. There is no need to explain how since centuries thieves or goons loot the wealthy through finding out about their resources.

Q: *Whether the valuation of the property and 20 percent more value are not a way for forcible sale of property. Is not it an insult to person, violation of freedom and dictatorship?*

A. We must protect the dignity and freedom of the citizens. At the same time, we should also respect the truth and understand the subtle difference between liberty and arrogance. This is neither an insult to the citizen nor violation of their freedom and a dictatorship. It has purpose to protect everyone's respect, freedom and equality. All of these will be equal for all. Freedom means freedom to speak the truth, not to untruth. Isn't it a borader freedom when property owner will be given right to evaluate their own property. Some specific laws will come into materialization only when another member of the society is prepared to pay at least 20 percent more than the value estimated by him. If owner is willing to sell its property on low price, none should have objection on it. Something wrong? Yes. The present system for property value assessment is completely wrong. In fact, it is an open fraud with the society that should be ended immediately.

Q. Why do you think it is necessary to draw Line of Wealth Line, introducing tax on excessive property, and sharing dividend among the all citizens?

A. A best question indeed! This system is not only necessary for justice but also for ensuring happiness, peace, prosperity and security. The economic justice system is also for eliminating poverty, unemployment, inflation, corruption, helplessness and many other kinds of conflicts from society. Goodwill, faith, love, truth, co-operation is absolutely necessary for a happy and peaceful society.

Moreover, the most important side is the principle of circulation of money that is the key to prosperity, happiness and peace. Lakshmi, which is considered goddess of wealth in Hinduism, is awesome, and it never stays at one place. Similarly, money should circulate constantly. Its stagnation is a curse for society according to Hinduism as well as in the economy that exists like a cycle of stream flow.

Sea is the largest water body, in which all the rivers keep on submerge. Sea has cycle of evaporation of water into clouds, and thereafter raining that becomes streams and sweet water reservoirs, finally the streams (rivers) submerge with Sea. Rain greens earth and rain water supports life. This cycle of water keeps on. Honestly, there is no short age of water anywhere, but wheresoever this cycle is disturbed, water scarcity and drought happens. The circulation of money and wealth is like this natural cycle of water. Due to the emergence of small monetary sources and hubs, the money continues to flow towards the larger sources; however unlike water cycle it gets accumulated by the wealthy and gets stagnant within certain class. It in fact should reach to the people like water cycle. The distribution of dividend to all the people of the country is an attempt similar to the cycle of water on the earth. A dividend is not a reward or wages; it is a kind of bonus from the natural resources on which everyone has equal right. The dividend is a just share of a person. If we do not implement taxed earnings from excessive wealth, we will shake religious commandments, ethics and belief in humanity. Nothing can be saved without it. Everything will be destroyed. Only silence of cemetery will prevail.

Q: One-tax system based on economic justice will be easily accepted by the poor; however why should the rich accept it. Their benefit?

A. I think rich will get the benefit more than their imagination. Besides, entire society will consider them a source of income generation. Poor will not even think of doing wrong against them. Despite poor will protect them, and will offer their lives to defend them. They respect them and will keep them at high esteem.

Rich will get rid of many obstacles in their business. Government's illegitimate interferences and lethargies will end. They will get rid of all kinds of extortions and insults. Market will be liberated and rivalries end. A free use of money will emerge, and opportunities and compatibilities will be the in unison with the competence. They will get rid of the compulsion, fear, tension and guilt of untruth. There will be no threat to their sustenance. An unnecessary laborious accounts keeping will end. Their security will be unchallenged, and extra protection plans will end. This will give them a real freedom.

Citizens will demand to elect the Senators (Member Rajiya Sabha in India) among the high tax payers and experts. They can contribute new ideas based on their contribution, and make appropriate laws for prosperous and happy country. And, the society will be grateful for this to them. They will be honored with the most prestigious national awards and titles. Their wealth will change into happiness. How valuable are these advantages. Again, they will get beyond their imagination.